Prague 2001

The Municipal House of the City of Prague

> 1

The Municipal House
of the City of Prague

1 > Ladislav Šaloun, Humiliation of the Nation

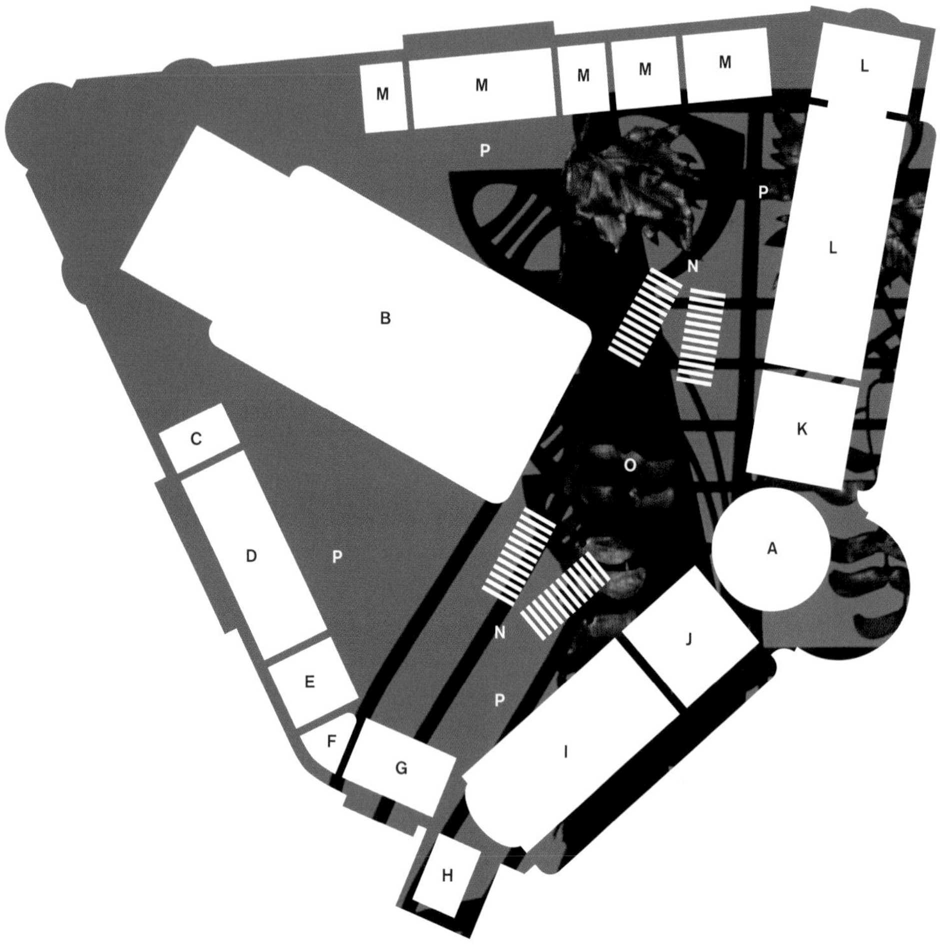

Ground plan of the Municipal House and legend to the halls and parlors on the first floor

A > Mayor's Hall
B > Smetana Hall
C > Orchestra Conductor's Apartment
D > Confectionery
E > Moravian Slovakian Parlor
F > Božena Němcová Parlor
G > Oriental Parlor
H > Clubroom in the corridor to the Powder Tower
I > Grégr Hall
J > Palacký Hall
K > Riegr Hall
L > Sladkovský Hall
M > Dining Parlors and adjoining parlors
N > Main Stairway
O > Foyer on the first floor
P > Corridors on the first floor

ISBN: 80-86339-11-4 (English)
ISBN: 80-86339-10-6 (Czech)

Municipal House

Exteriors

Ground Floor

Basement

Raised Ground Floor

First Floor

Mezzanine

Second Floor

New Rooms

Forward

Dear visitors of Prague,
after seeing the captivating panorama of the Prague Castle and Lesser Town, walking through Petřín park and visiting Vyšehrad, you are possibly convinced that you have already experienced the best that Prague has to offer. But while wandering through the historical streets of Old Town, a large and glowing, richly decorated palace appears before you in a completely unexpected place – the Municipal House of the City of Prague. Connected to the Powder Tower, which at one time served as the main entry to the city, and hidden in a labyrinth of buildings, each of which was constructed in a different era and architectural style. The Prague city council decided to build its ceremonial building at the beginning of the last century, and it was meant to be proof and a calling card for the technical, artistic, artisanal, and cultural maturity of the nation. The place selected for the construction had been the location of the Old Town, early Gothic fortifications from the middle of the 13th century. In 1383, Václav IV. moved his residence from the Prague Castle here to King's Court. Zikmund Lucemburský, Albrecht II. Habsburg, Ladislav Pohrobek, and Jiří of Poděbrady also administered the Czech lands from here. The coronation and funeral processions of the rulers to St. Vitus' Cathedral at the Prague Castle also began here, to ask for God's favor and forgiveness. It was Vladislav II. Jagelonský who moved his seat back to the Prague Castle in 1484. King's Court gradually changed into a seminary and military barracks, which were torn down in 1902–1903, as were the classicist shops a year later.
In a memorial letter on October 10, 1901, the administrative committee of the Civic League (Měšťanská beseda) urged the township of Prague to aid in the construction of a new building, which would serve as its ceremonial building and house the abundantly expanded group activities of the time. After much negotiation, on January 5, 1903, the board of town elders of the city administration decided to buy a large parcel of land next to the Powder Tower from the Entrepreneurial Bank (Živnostenská banka), and there construct the Municipal House. In spite of the poor state of city finances at the time, the city representatives approved its construction. They wanted to create a dignified presentation of Czech culture in a place, memorable for the nation, which was neglected at the turn of the 20th century and gradually abandoned by the inhabitants of Prague.
Unsatisfied with the results of the architectural competition for the Municipal House project, the board of town elders decided to award the project to the architects Antonín Balšánek and Osvald Polívka.
Construction began on August 21, 1905, and the building was gradually brought into usage towards the end of 1911. The Municipal House was opened to the general public on January 5, 1912, and became a symbol of the consciousness of Czech ethnicity, not only in Prague, but throughout the entire country.
In the decades that followed, the Municipal House began to live the fortunes of its nation, and its very space played a key role during the preparation for and declaration of the independent Czechoslovak Republic in 1918. The splendor and beauty of the Municipal House seemed to reflect the economic growth and energy of the newly formed state. After the German occupation in 1939, memorial plaques and inscriptions reminiscent of the steps of the nation on the path to freedom were either hidden from the view of the public or removed entirely. Many of them remained "lost" throughout long decades. After the Second World War, the Municipal House no longer lived up to its pre-war beauty and renown. Even so, it played host to almost all the world-renowned performers of classical music. The second half of the 20th century meant a gradual decline for the Municipal House, similar to the decline of the economic and cultural prestige of the nation and the country. In 1989 it once again served as the location of the first official negotiations between the deposed political powers and their successors. The building was returned to the ownership of the capital city Prague in an extremely bad state. In the first half of the nineties, Prague's elected representatives decided to completely restore the building and its artistic decoration to its former state, and so the Municipal House enters the 21st century in all of its beauty and splendor, ready to greet home and foreign visitors to the capital city.

František Laudát > Director of the Municipal House

KOMERČNÍ
SYMFONICKÝ ORCHESTR HL. M. PRAHY
PRAGUE SYMPHONY ORCHESTRA
fok

Permanent Exhibition in the Open Air

The monumental structure of the Municipal House forms a large, independent, and compact block of an irregular triangular shape. The main façade is vaulted with a dome above. The façade has a broken front to the main bay, which gives the impression of a symmetrical layout for the whole building. Despite the fact that it is a multi-purpose building, we can say, with a bit of exaggeration, that as a whole, it looks like a luxurious, large Art-Nouveau "villa" with only two stories. The five large, functional stories open to the public (in fact, there are seven stories total, including two service floors) are thus craftily disguised. The spacious exhibition halls, for instance, are inconspicuously inserted in the garret, the huge halls of the Pilsen Restaurant and Wine Bar are located in the basement, and the luxurious concert hall is surrounded by rows of halls, parlors and other rooms on several floors, often even in multiple rows.

Standing right outside the Municipal House entrance, visitors can appreciate the picture completed by the marquee and colored stained-glass panes bordering the main curve of the concave aedicule of the middle part of the bay with a balcony. The marquee is supported by stone pillars with bronze figures of torchbearers by Karel Novák. The curve of the balcony is bordered by a finely crafted railing with botanical as well as floral motifs, and the coat-of-arms of the city of Prague in the central cartouche.

The triaxial portal composition of the main entrance is situated under the balcony. The triple entrance doors with glass panes and brass Art-Nouveau door handles stand between a pair of square pillars. The fanlight is decorated with geometrical colored stained glass. Three window openings into the Mayor's Hall are centrally situated above the balcony. Polychrome coats-of-arms of historic Prague towns in the bay of the architrave are another part of the decorative composition of the façade. The continuous entablature is broken along the main axis by a lambrequin-shaped pediment with a pair of torches.

The vertical composition culminates in a semicircular gable with a tympanum decorated with a distinctive mosaic, by Karel Špillar, called the "Apotheosis of Prague". It is a glass mosaic marked by a harmonic balance of gold and pastel hues.

The impression is intensified by the inscription in the bordering stripe of the archivolt: "Hail to you, Prague! Stand up to the wrath of time as well as you have resisted all storms throughout the ages!" In the archivolt springer there are two male mascarons, and the top is decorated by a cartouche with multi-color coats-of-arms of the city of Prague, situated in a gable which carries a symbol of the Czech crown.

The lunette composition is complemented by sculptures to each side by Ladislav Šaloun, called "Humiliation of the Nation" and "Resurrection of the Nation". The mass of the main façade is concentrated in the copper dome set on a circular tambour. The ribs between the glass-filled surfaces are finished by mascarons at the points where they touch the tambour. The dome culminates in an elaborately constructed lantern.

The side wings of the façade have an uneven number of window axes. The left wing has six axes and a vaulted above-ground corridor to the Powder Tower. The right wing has seven axes, finishing in a one-axis, three-story-high corner bay. The ground floor, with rustication, holds the windows of the Café and the French Restaurant. These sash windows are articulated by vertical bars and impressively glazed with beveled clear and frosted glass.

Above the ground floor, a row of pairs of corbels support a balcony that stretches along both wings of the building. Under the balcony, large outdoor spherical lights are hung. During the construction of the building, these lights had the significance of providing ceremonial lighting, independent of the gloomy streets. The iron railing is a striking Art-Nouveau decorative feature of the balcony. It consists of flowing curves, which wind among botanical and floral motifs. The balcony is connected to the outer walls by constructions of poles with lights. The high semicircular windows of the first floor are optically separated by pilasters whose capitals are filled with medallions showing different types of Czech costumes, designed by Josef Pekárek, Augustin Zoula, Edouard Pikart and Antonín Štrunc. The fifteen window openings of the front façade of the second floor are bordered by linear molding with top voussoirs, which are realized as interesting mascarons of decoratively symbolic meaning. These mascarons, created by Karel Novák, are unique, artistically remarkable stucco sculptures

> 4

2 << Main entrance
3 << Balcony above the main entrance with the coat-of-arms of Prague and Torchbearers by Karel Novák
4 << Above-ground corridor to the Powder Tower, in the corner niche a statue of Matěj Rejsek by Čeněk Vosmík

5 > Commemorative plaque about the events of 1918 by Ladislav Šaloun
6 > Main marquee

> 5

of heads, complemented with stylized attributes of various branches of human activities, such as painting, philosophy, business, agriculture, industry, and even then-arising fields like motoring or aeronautics.

The console above the voussoir is a part of the striking linear molding of the architrave of the running entablature, which carries a parapet with semicircular roof, articulated by stripes and tiled with ceramic roof tiles with green glazing. These green roof tiles, combined with brown ones, make a decorative stripe above the parapet.

The corner of the left wing is emphasized by rich sculptural decoration along its entire height. An allegorical figure of an angel by František Rous, called "Spirit of the History", is sitting above the main cornice. The figure of the famous architect Matěj Rejsek, by Čeněk Vosmík, is standing on the first floor, and under him, on the ground floor, there is another corner bronze plaque with two shield-bearers, made by Ladislav Šaloun in 1931. It was removed at the order of the Protectorate officials during the night from April 3 to April 4, 1940, because it was a reminder of the declaration of the independent republic in 1918.

The right-corner bay disrupts the running line of the roof and culminates in an independent helm roof with broach posts. They are connected by gilded decorative grill. In the window axis, the entablature of the right wing turns into a lambrequin-shaped pediment, adorned with a cartouche with stylized Art-Nouveau branches. Two allegorical sculptures of "Literature" and "Architecture", by Antonín Štrunc, sit on the side pedestals. Around the corner, on U Obecního domu Street, the bay is embellished with similar allegorical sculptures of "Sculpture" and "Painting".

On the sides of the building, the vertical and horizontal elements are designed in strict relation to each other. A greater emphasis is on the vertical rhythm through an accentuated plinth and mezzanine. The elevation up to the running fascia is textured. The fascia is broken by marquees above the side entrances of the bays.

The construction of a spectacular Art-Nouveau marquee is made of iron and glass with a decorative front of punched metal sheets. It is adorned by a garland of bulbs and is enhanced on the top by a lantern. This light decoration is particularly impressive in the evening.

The bays are enhanced by pilasters with empty medallions and, above the windows of the second mezzanine, by a relief of two sitting male figures with the representation of a lyre. The sculptures are twined with floral garlands with ribbons, which border the window segment up to the mezzanine.

The vertical orientation of the bays culminates in a series of tympanums, with archivolts decorated by mascarons of a girl's face and by reliefs of stylized, fan-shaped flowers. The tympanums are a part of a pyramid mansard roof. The rest of the elevation is articulated by lesenes with medallions of Czech folk costumes.

At the top, stucco centerpieces with Art-Nouveau decorations connect the windows. A balcony and decorative railing emphasize the central part of the side elevation above the mezzanine. The third row of windows is separated by a parapet stripe with sculpted ornamentation of symbolic emblems.

Dormer windows with spired helm roofs enhance the simple roof of the middle part.

The wooden shop windows of the stores on the ground floor were remodeled, according to period photographs, in order to resume function. The stores have been rented again to companies of famous brands with luxurious goods.

Similar to the front façade, here also a row of sconces in the shape of clear balls is situated under the cornice.

Both side elevations have almost an identical design, with the exception of the side face on U Prašné brány Street, where the link to the tower logically disturbs the rhythm of articulation. The large bay by the Powder Tower is enhanced by a balcony supported by corbels. The three-part balcony window of the first floor is adorned by pillars, which support the entablature with a couple of putti twined with a garland coming from the middle medallion. The pillars stretch to the higher floors, up to the top segmented window of the gable. They are linked by a botanical band with female mascarons at the level of the entablature.

The archivolt of the semicircular window is bordered by a molding of stylized leaves and fruit, connected by a cartouche at the top. Two alle-

Text on the Bronze Plaque Set on the Corner by the Powder Tower

THIS BUILDING, THE MUNICIPAL HOUSE OF THE CAPITAL CITY OF PRAGUE, WAS BLESSED BY THE CZECHOSLOVAK REVOLUTION. HERE, IN GRÉGR HALL, THE DECLARATION OF ALL THE NATION'S DEPUTIES WAS APPROVED ON JANUARY 6, 1918. HERE, IN SMETANA HALL, THE GLORIOUS OATH OF THE NATION WAS PLEDGED ON APRIL 13, 1918. HERE, THE CONFERENCE OF THE OPPRESSED NATIONS OF THE AUSTRO-HUNGARIAN EMPIRE TOOK PLACE ON MAY 17, 1918, AT THE TIME OF THE JUBILEE OF THE NATIONAL THEATER. HERE, IN GRÉGR HALL, THE CZECHOSLOVAK NATIONAL COMMITTEE WAS ESTABLISHED ON JULY 13, 1918. HERE, THE DAY OCTOBER 28, 1918, SPOKE AND ACTED. HERE, THE CHAIRMEN OF THE NATIONAL COMMITTEE GATHERED IN THE MORNING OF OCTOBER 28, 1918, TO EXECUTE A REVOLUTIONARY COUP D'ÉTAT IN THE NAME OF THE NATION, TO TAKE OVER THE PUBLIC ADMINISTRATION, AND TO PROCLAIM THE INDEPENDENCE OF THE CZECHOSLOVAK REPUBLIC. HERE, THE MILITARY FORCES OF THE HABSBURG EMPIRE SURRENDERED TO THE CZECHOSLOVAK REVOLUTION IN THE EVENING OF OCTOBER 28, 1918. HERE, THE NATIONAL COMMITTEE HAD ITS FIRST MEETINGS AS THE FIRST PARLIAMENT AND GOVERNMENT OF THE RE-ESTABLISHED STATE BETWEEN OCTOBER 28 AND NOVEMBER 13, 1918, AND HERE, THE REPUBLIC'S FIRST LAWS WERE PASSED. CZECHOSLOVAK PEOPLE, YOU, WHO TRAVEL PAST THIS BUILDING, REMEMBER FOREVER YOUR GREAT REVOLUTION AND THE SOLEMN DUTIES TO YOUR FREEDOM.

gorical "half-figures" of a "Sower" and "Harvester" by Antonín Mára are placed on the sides of the bay's segmented gable.

The rear central bay, in a cylindrical form of an outside corner, concentrates the mass of both side wings. Two interesting sculptures of "Bagpiper" and "Water Fairy" by František Uprka are placed on brackets in the middle of the face height. The dome roofing of the bay is surrounded by luxurious allegories of "Drama" and "Music" by Josef Mařatka. The front of the ground floor is enhanced by an entry portal with a huge sopraporta. The archivolt is decorated by a couple of putti with an elaborate garland, which is at the peak connected with a mascaron of a female head with flowers and fruit. The round corner bay is topped by a ribbed dome on a tambour, which allows a view of a gable in the roof above Smetana Hall, with a large semicircular window. Today this gable houses the Orchestra Conductor's Apartment.

The above-ground corridor connecting the Municipal House and the Powder Tower by Antonín Štrunc and Josef Pekárek is another distinctive, interesting, and inseparable part of the building of the Municipal House. The design implements a combination of renaissance and Art-Nouveau details. The building of sandstone masonry is made to match the tower. The semicircular tunnel vault of the passage is ornamented with arch rings, which spring from the pillars of the load-bearing walls of both connected buildings. In the right lunette of the passage, a geometrically segmented window was made. The arcade front of the top of the passage is embellished by an Art-Nouveau cartouche with an oval coat-of-arms of the city of Prague with the inscription "PRAGA CAPUT REGNI".

The first floor of the connecting corridor, which is linked to Grégr Hall, is accentuated by three arches on Tuscan orders. In the side segments, relief male half-figures and grotesque figures on both sides of the voussoir catch the eye of the passer-by. The pillar parapet of the terrace above the arches allows entrance to the first floor of the tower. The top of the parapet is decorated by typical Art-Nouveau ornaments and by a stripe of emblems of the Czech lands and royal cities. A part of the connecting corridor is also a small oriel window by the Gothic scroll of the side wall of the tower.

> 6

> 7

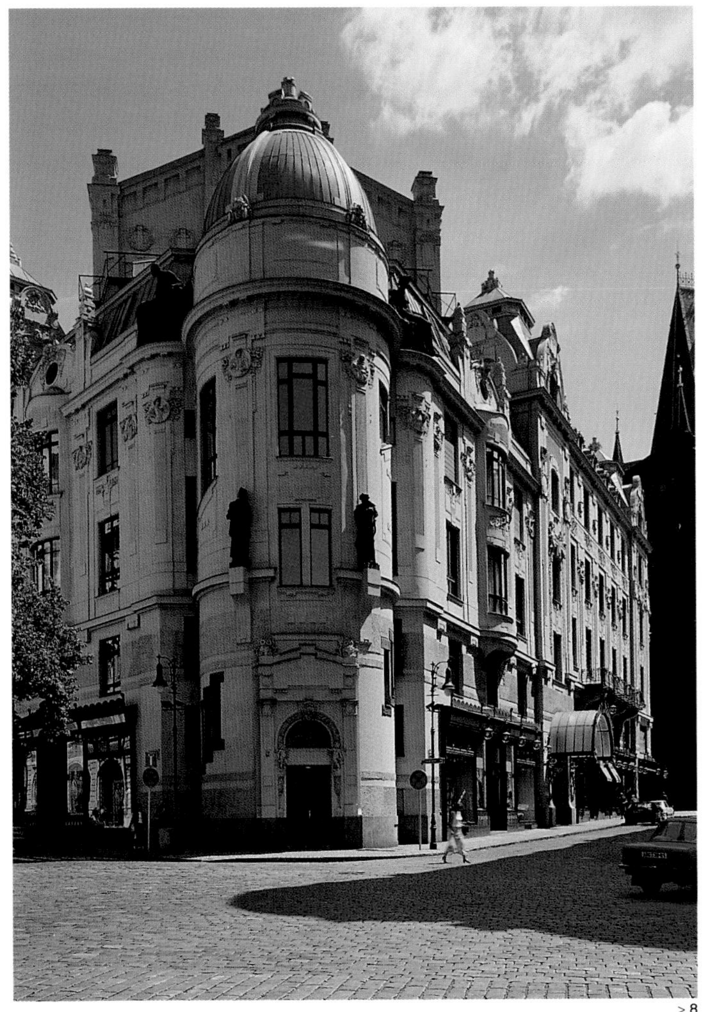

> 8

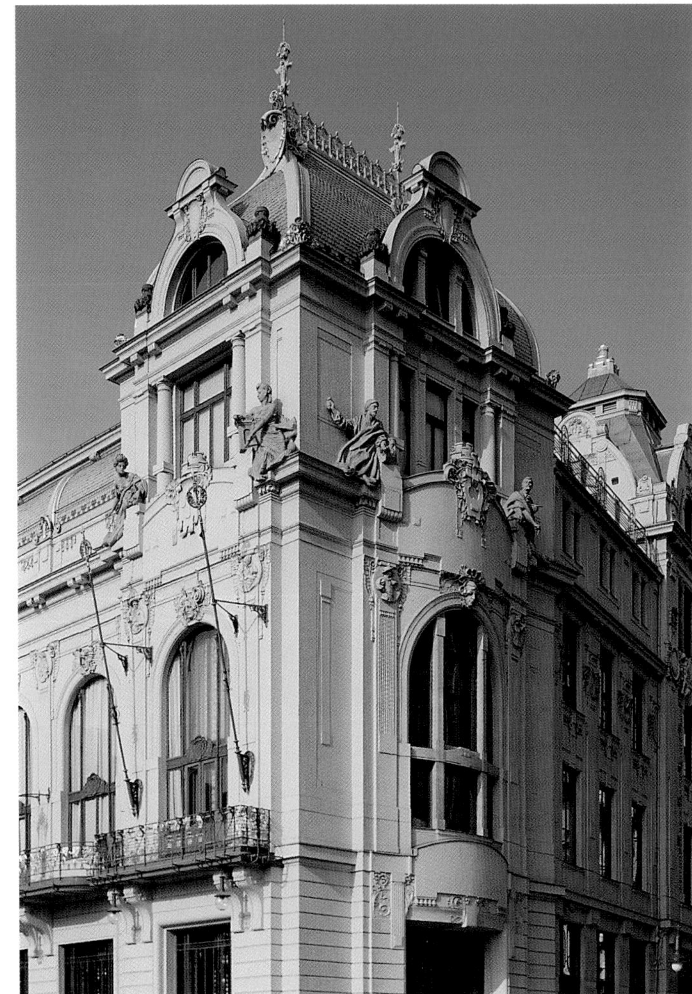

> 9

7 < Main façade

8 > Rear entrance with sculptures by František Uprka a Josef Mařatka

9 > Corner with allegorical sculptures by Antonín Štrunc

ZDAR TOBE PRAHO! VZDORUJ CASU ZLOBE
JAK ODOLALAS

10 < The top part of the main façade with the mosaic picture of the Apotheosis of Prague by Karel Špillar and sculptures by Ladislav Šaloun

> 10

> 11

ZDAR TOBE PRAHO VZDORUJ CASU ZLOBE
JAK ODOLALAS VEKY BOURIM VSEM

> 12

> 13

> 14

11 < Ladislav Šaloun, Humiliation of the Nation

12 < Karel Špillar, Apotheosis of Prague and the Prague coat-of-arms

13 > František Rous, Spirit of History

14 > František Rous, Spirit of History

> 15

15–18 > Sculpted decoration of side and rear elevations

> 16

> 17

> 18

19 > Karel Novák, Aeronautics (allegorical head)
20 > František Uprka, Bagpiper
21 > Decoration of the side elevation

> 19

> 20

22 > Elevation of the U Obecního domu Street

23 > Karel Novák, Torchbearer (in front of the balcony outside the Mayor's Hall)

> 22

24 > Main marquee, detail
25 > Top of the marquee of a side entrance
26 > Stained glass of the main entrance marquee

> 24

> 25

> 26

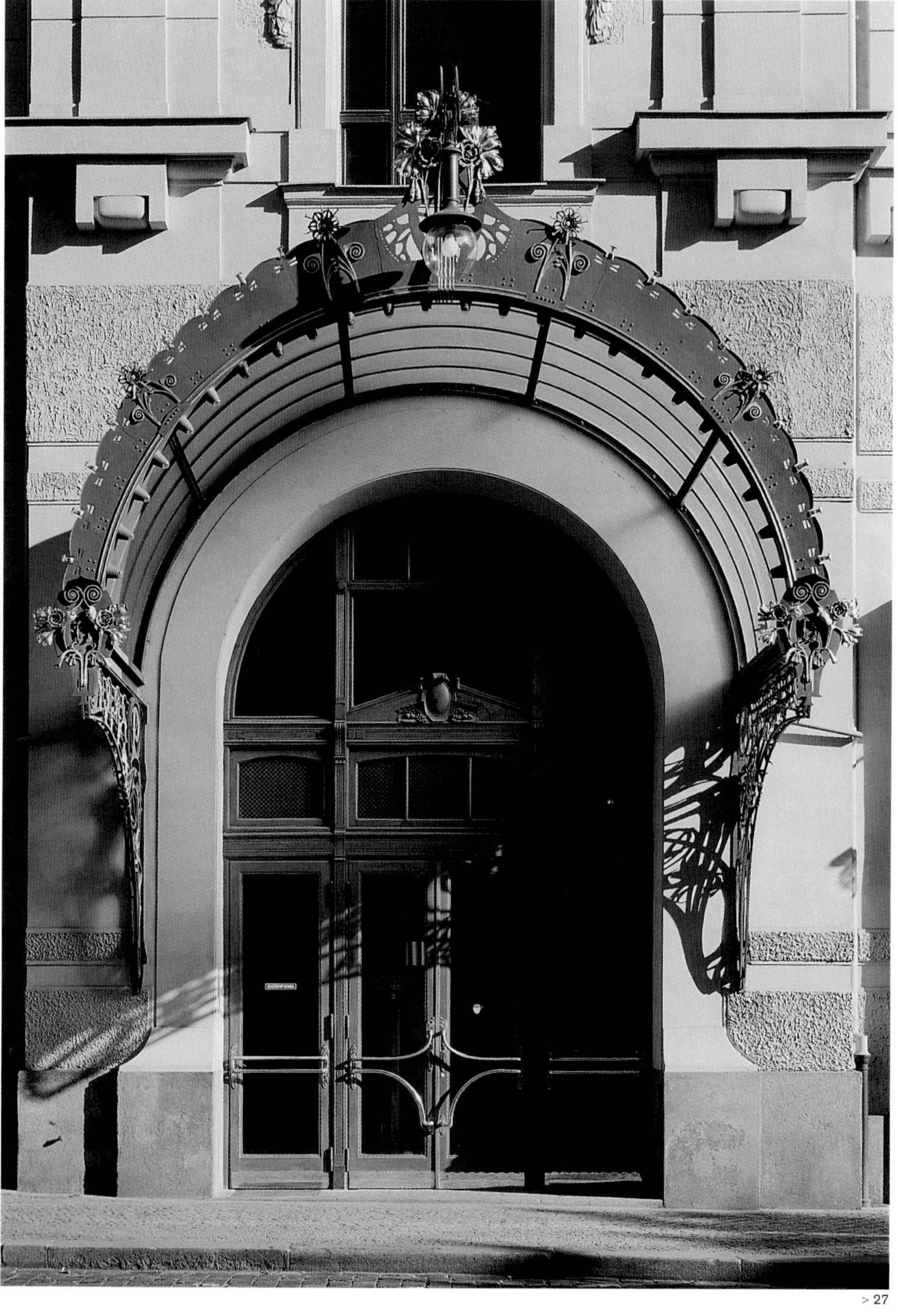

> 27

27 < Side entrance marquee
28–30 > Details of railings and marquees

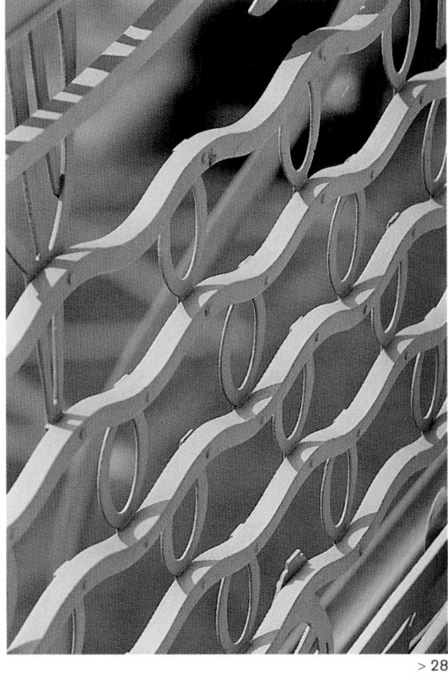
> 28

> 29

> 30

31–33 > Railings of balconies
34 > Bracket of a side entrance marquee

> 31

> 32

> 33

> 35

35 > Roof with rooflights
36 > Bottom part of the main dome

> 37

> 38

> 39

37–41 > Main dome decoration
42 > Roof decoration above the corner of U Obecního domu Street, with a window to an exhibition hall

43 >> Coat-of-arms of the City of Prague at the top of the main gable
44 >> Ladislav Šaloun, Resurrection of the Nation

> 40

> 41

> 42

> 43

BOURIM VSEM!

> 45

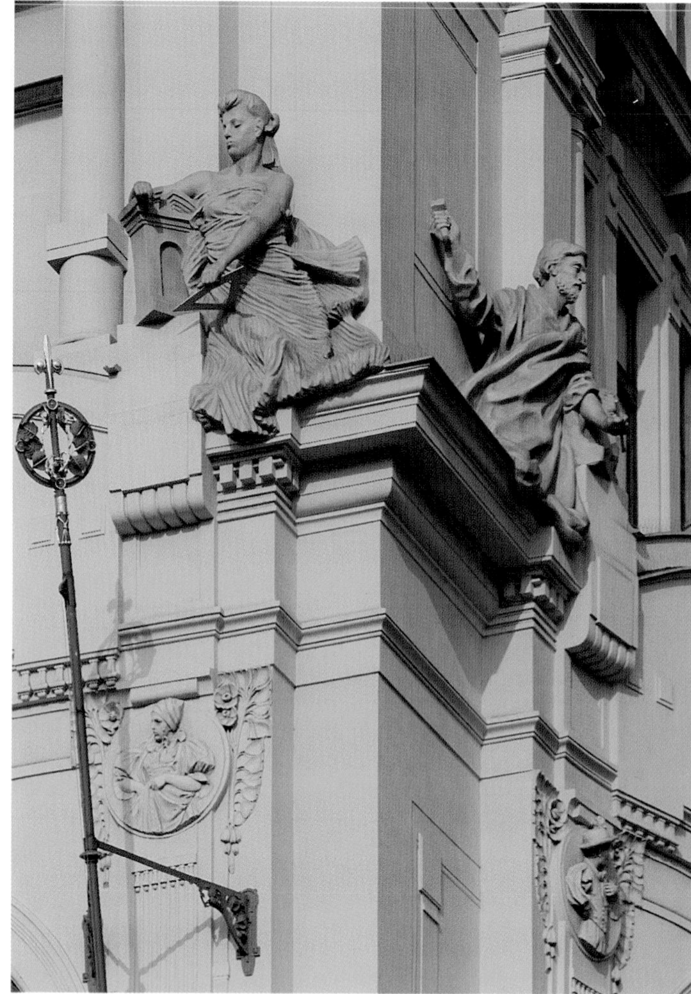

> 46

45 > Antonín Štrunc, Literature

46 > Antonín Štrunc, Architecture, Sculpture

47 > Josef Mařatka, Drama

> 48

48 > Karel Novák, Torchbearer

49 > The main balcony with the coat-of-arms of the Old Town, above it the coats-of-arms of other historical Prague towns

Entrance Hall

The starting point of the ground floor is the entrance hall. It is circular in shape and situated in the axis of the east façade's bend. It is the main vertical, in fact central, axis of the building. However, compared to the imaginary geometrical center of the large building, it is shifted one window bay to the left. Even so, especially as viewed from the front, it represents the central axis of the building according to its irregular floor plan. The main entrance and balcony, as well as the marquee and dome, are all situated in the main axis.

The entrance to the Municipal House is through a triple-arch doorway which is partly hidden from view by a richly decorated marquee and only after entering through the entrance hall can one appreciate the richness of the stained glass in the door as well as on the semicircular fanlights. Any careful visitor will not miss the richly decorated Art-Nouveau iron door fittings.

The entrance hall interior is surprisingly high, stretching up the height of both the ground floor and the mezzanine. It has an elliptical dome with oval lunettes above the arcades of the entrance portals. In relation to the lunettes, the surface of the vaulting is emphasized by ornamental plaster. The arcade above the entrance to the stairway hall is skirted by a band of stucco decoration of Art-Nouveau-shaped, coiled lime branches. A cartouche with the coat-of-arms of the city of Prague is situated in the peak of the ceiling. Two semicircular stained-glass windows, located right under the vault, lead to the balconies of the side halls, the Pilsen Restaurant, and the Café. The walls of the pillars and the niches are decorated with marble wainscoting and, on the bottom part, with a running plinth of the same material. Black marble panels with the names of the halls on the right and left sides of the building are situated along the sides of the entrance door wall, towards the central foyer and the cloakroom. Above these panels are bronze reliefs of reclining figures by Bohumil Kafka named "Fauna" and "Flora", whose quality is quite good for the time at which they were made. Both of the side doorways (along the lateral axis) lead to the large halls of the Pilsen Restaurant and the Café. Another impressive feature is the door portals with the sopraportas embellished by stucco lime branches. Above them, in the upper part, is a lunette with a colorful stained-glass window. The entrance door, a swing door with beveled glass panels, has beautifully twisted wooden handles with brass fixtures.

Opposite the entrance portal, there is a large oak wall with doors. It features a large number of glass panes and a basket-shaped fanlight. It provides access to the ceremonial halls of the building – except for the Pilsen Restaurant and the Café which have side entrances from this entrance hall, as mentioned above. The front wall is modestly adorned with a carved garland of branches and an inscription: "MUNICIPAL HOUSE HALLS".

The floor of the circular entrance hall is also artistically quite impressive. The symmetrical composition of mosaic marble tiling with purfle was created by Giovanni Petrucci. The dominating white color in the ornaments, as complemented by the pink, grayish-green, ochre, and gray, creates a ceremonial atmosphere for the whole entrance hall.

Wall fixtures with lusters as well as the modern and stylish radiator covers complete the image of the circular entrance hall and make it a full-fledged hall of the Municipal House.

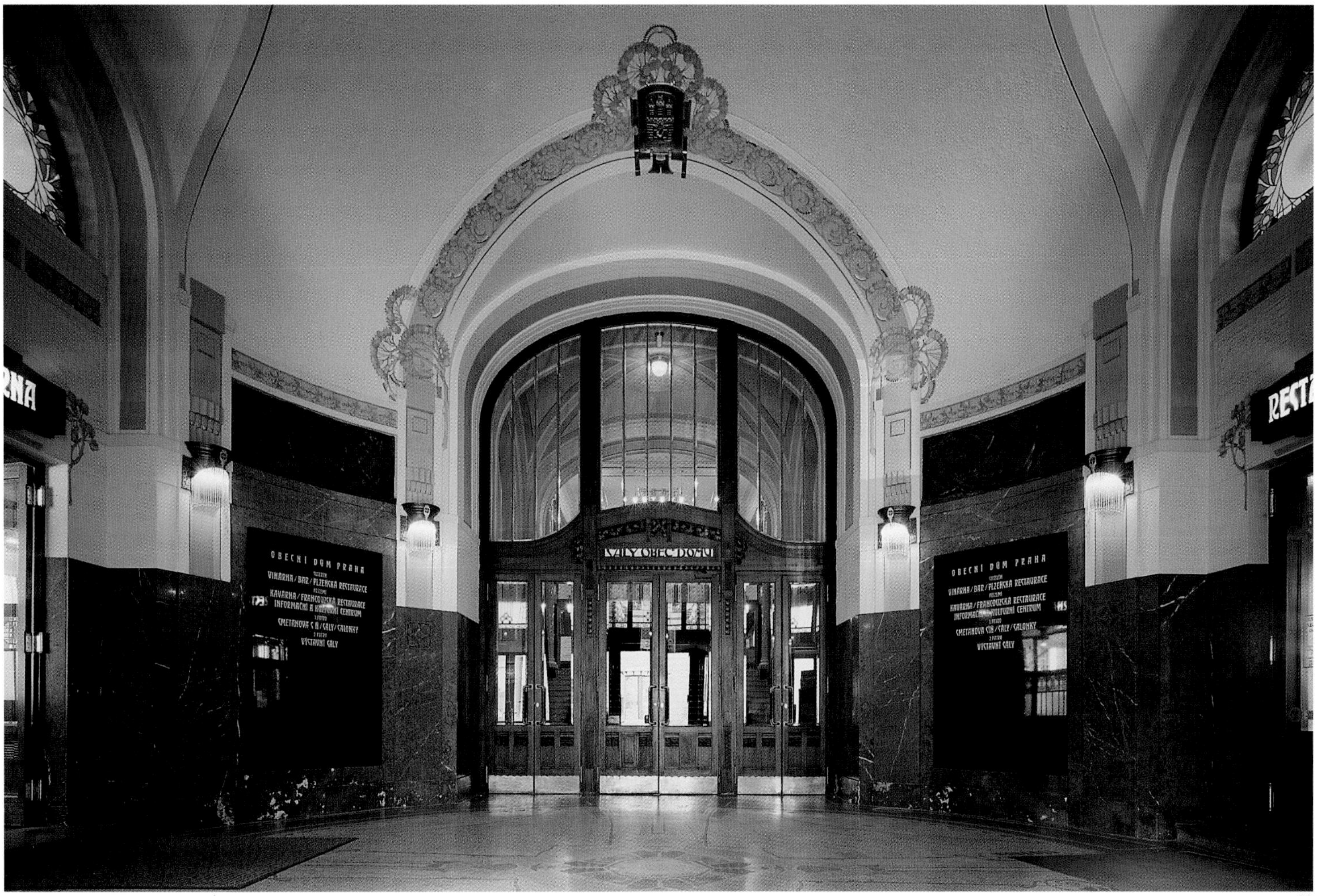
OBECNÍ DŮM PRAHA
VINÁRNA / BAR / PLZEŇSKÁ RESTAURACE
KAVÁRNA / FRANCOUZSKÁ RESTAURACE
SMETANOVA SÍŇ / SÁLY / SALONKY
VÝSTAVNÍ SÁLY

> 50

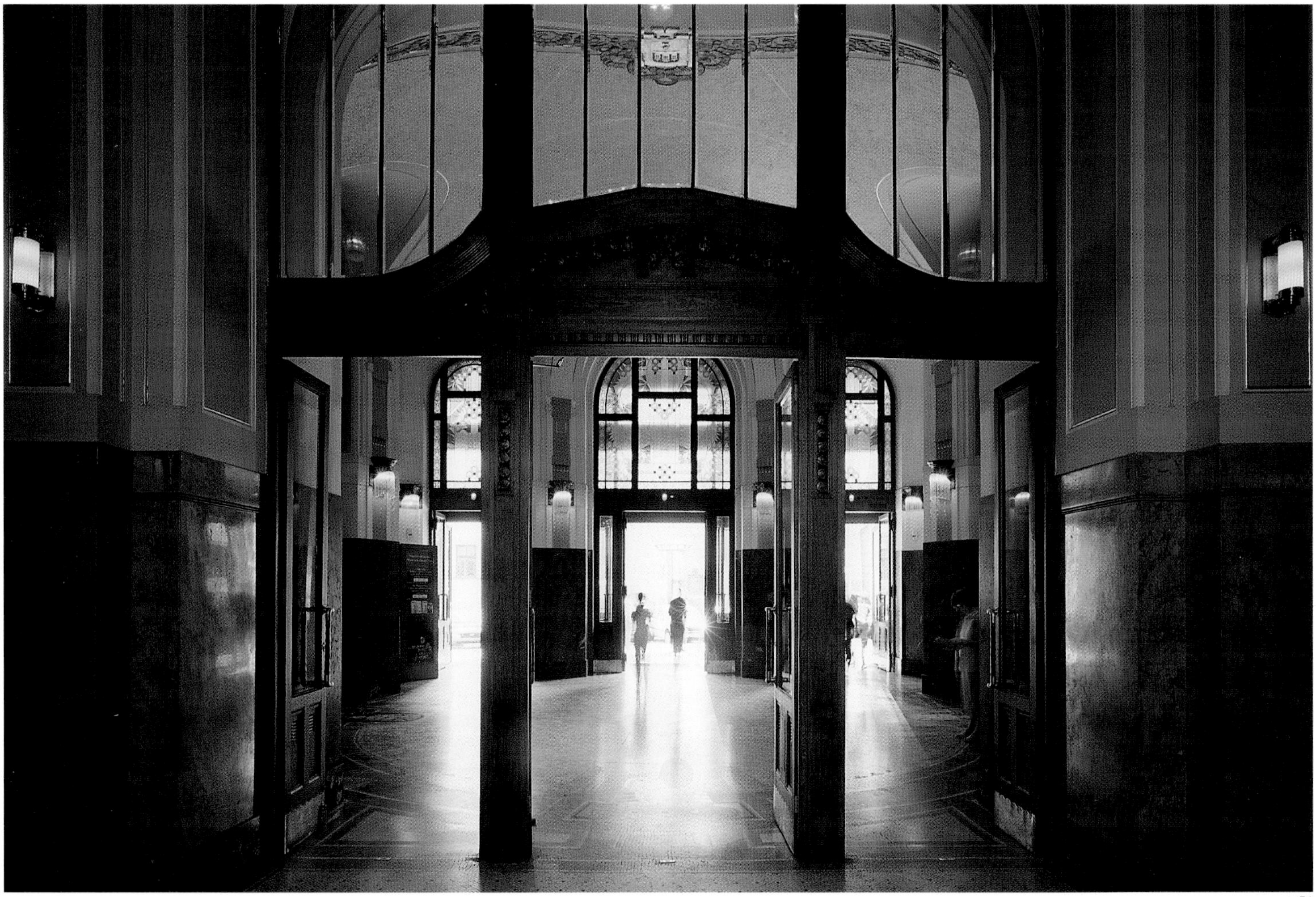

> 51

50 << Entrance hall towards the stairway, reliefs of Fauna and Flora by Bohumil Kafka on the sides
51 << View from the stairway towards the main entrance

52 > Bohumil Kafka, Flora
53 > Coat-of-arms of Prague above the doorway to the stairway
54 > Entrance to the Café

> 52

> 53

> 54

Café

To the left of the entrance hall there is the large "Café" occupying all of the ground floor of the left wing. It was designed in such a way that a guest sitting in a typical café-style chair felt more like in a Prague street of the time than in a vast impersonal hall. This effect is made possible by unusually large windows, with beveled glass panes in close proximity to one another. This window wall connects the interior with the exterior not only optically and impressively, but the large sash windows, when opened, eliminate the imaginary border of the building. During the summer season two of the sills under the windows can be removed and the Café can be thus connected with the street or front garden directly. Tables placed in the street enlarge the café's space.

The longitudinal hall of the Café has six axes and a flat ceiling. The long walls are articulated by ranks of pillars. A mezzanine balcony, situated on the right side, opposite the window wall, has a parapet consisting of segmented sections. A balcony lies above the main entrance into the Café, supported by a couple of small pillars, which leads into the gallery.

Unlike in the French Restaurant, the grid of joists corresponds to the supporting system of the perimeter pillars. The joists divide the ceiling into segments with stucco ovals, whose circumference is bordered by sculpted molding. The ovals are set in rectangular frames, formed by the joists, decorated by coffers, and connecting bands, with circular gilded centers and stripes of stylized cable molding.

The wall segments are articulated by simple rectangular frames of egg molding, which also borders the balcony parapets. Sopraportas decorated with rhomboids and ovals populate the lower part of the pillars above the mirrors. The motif of panels with rhomboids can be also found on the parapets of the north balcony and gallery.

A lighted fountain and a relief of a "Nymph" by Josef Pekárek lie underneath the exedra of the front wall, also quite structurally complex, complete with a lunette. The bottom part of the fountain, made of Carrara marble, is convex in shape between two blocks of socle. A concavely scalloped tabernacle acts as a base to a molded panel with a relief, under which three brass spouts bring the water. The fountain wall is at the bottom wainscoted with green marble, vertically decorated by wrought brass meanders and articulated by floral jardinière with decorative grills. The top part of the exedra is adorned with stucco tile pattern with gilded centers. The archivolte of the arcade is bordered by gilded cable molding and dentil. Above the fountain, a decorative brass grill is situated. The top of the lunette is ornate with a geometrical stucco decoration. The whole wall of the exedra is adorned with chessboard-like squares shaped to fit the curve of the wall. The portal curve is flanked by a band of diamond-shaped elements with gilded disks. In the bottom part, marble wainscoting of a different hue of green links the exedra to the fountain and is articulated by vertical brass stripes.

It is interesting to note that the opposite wall, whose entrance, balcony, and pillars are wainscoted with green marble, separates the entrance space from the side parlors in a striking way. A band of rectangular brass grills runs under the balcony parapet. A pair of candelabrum lighting units forms a unique artistic accent on the face of the balcony. Wooden rods running in front of small pillars continue up a runged brass structure to the ceiling of the hall where they then converge on the balcony in a trio of lights. The structure is complemented with a brass octagon of a clock, embellished with colored glass lenses. It hangs on a strut between both lighting units.

The entrance space under the balcony is articulated by wooden coffered walls to create two side parlors with colored stained-glass panes in a rectangular grid of brass frames, with geometrical diamond-shaped diagrams. A double swinging door with twisted door handles and vision panels protected by geometrical brass grill hangs in the entry area. The ceilings of the parlors have simple frame molding with gilded bead molding. The brass oval lighting structure, with geometrical motifs, is flanked by two lights with glass lusters.

The brass structures of huge lights, hanging in two rows from the joists, are exceptionally elaborate. Suspended bars carry a pyramidal four-sided chandelier structure with brass rings of alternating octagonal lanterns and crystal lusters. A cylinder composed of long crystal chains and lusters hangs from the center of the chandelier. The lights were designed

55 << Fountain with a Nymph by Josef Pekárek

by the František Křižík company, which supplied all of the lighting units in the Café.

The sides of the hall are wainscoted with mahogany panels, into which pillar mirrors, leather-upholstered banquettes, built-in cabinets, and the window seats of the booths are inserted. Alongside the mirrors, original columns of lights with bulbs are attached. The wainscoting of the oval platform around the fountain is also quite elaborate. It is inlaid and ends in small pillars with brass lighting units.

The left outer wall between the pillars is filled with a structure of geometrically articulated sash windows, as mentioned above, with colorless and frosted beveled glass panes. The chain control of the vertical movement of the lower frame is hidden behind the wooden panel of the pillar. The wooden panels of the radiator covers under the windows are filled out with punch-cut brass sheets.

Furnishing in the Café consists of both rectangular and round tables made of rare green marble mounted on wooden cylindrical table bases, the bottom part of which is plated with brass sheets. The tables are complemented by elegant inlaid chairs, replicas of the original ones of which only a few specimens were preserved. Both the original chairs and the replicas were made by the Viennese firm Thonet.

The floor is covered by new crimson linoleum that is of the same color and similar quality as the original one from the time of the Café's opening in 1912. Preserving the original colors and structure of the items, which are liable to frequent changes and fashion aberrations, represents an important link to both the authenticity of the room and the impression it makes on the visitor. It is only in this way that the halls of the Municipal House can be viewed through the eyes and aesthetics of the period of its construction.

Along the right side of the room there is a cloakroom for the visitors to the Café hidden behind dominant pillars. There is also a horse-shoe shaped stairway leading down into the Wine Bar and up into the mezzanine gallery. Bands articulate the lowered ceiling into sections that are decorated by linear cornices with cable molding. When looking from below, the use of gilded plastic octagons and rhomboids is apparent. On the left side of the cloakroom, inlaid cabinets with marble tops and attached shelves are built into the paneling. The entrance to the stairway is separated by a three-part wooden structure reaching to the ceiling. The small pillars of the wall are inlaid, the fanlights are filled with grill. Above the stairway there is a mezzanine separated by a three-part wooden structure with glass-panel door and a middle panel with stained glass enhanced with geometrical patterns of green and yellow hues.

The Café's gallery, harmonized with the basic tectonic system of the hall, is articulated into four ceiling sections, whose stripes are along the width of the pillars enhanced with rectangles. Along the walls there are rectangular brass lighting units with two lights. The sections are decorated with moldings with small oval or rectangular patterns. The round lights in the center of each section have a load-bearing brass cylinder with a central light, which carries a brass ring with eight lights.

The gallery walls are frame-paneled with wallpaper inserts. Mirrors with wooden boxes with green marble tops are built into the paneling of the pillars. The booths in the pillar niches are furnished with upholstered banquettes with backs and tables with green marble tops.

An enhancing feature of the Café balcony is its semicircular, colored stained-glass window, which when viewed from the other side is a top window of the entrance hall. The walls are wainscoted, with built-in cabinets enhanced by brass grill. The balcony parapet has green marble wainscoting.

The Café as a whole is a ceremonial hall of the Municipal House which, thanks to its high standard and all-day service, used to be and still is a popular meeting place for both tourists and citizens of Prague of all ages.

56 > Vestibule

> 57

57 < View from the fountain towards the Café's entrance from the entrance hall

> 58

> 59

58 < Hangers of the Café's cloakroom

59 > Inlaid mahogany wainscoting

> 60

60 < Standing lamp on the booth by the fountain

61–64 > Lights

> 61

> 62

> 63

> 64

> 65

> 66

65 < The top part of a chandelier suspension
66 < Light on a gallery beam
67 > Light on the gallery
68 > Main chandelier, detail
69 > Wall-fitted column of lights

> 67

> 68

> 69

70–72 > Lights

73 > Reflection in a mirror, with bordering columns of lights

> 70

> 71

> 72

74 < View of the Café's front wall

> 74

> 75

75 < Balcony above the Café's entrance

76 > Railing of the balcony next to the window

77 > On the balcony

> 76

> 77

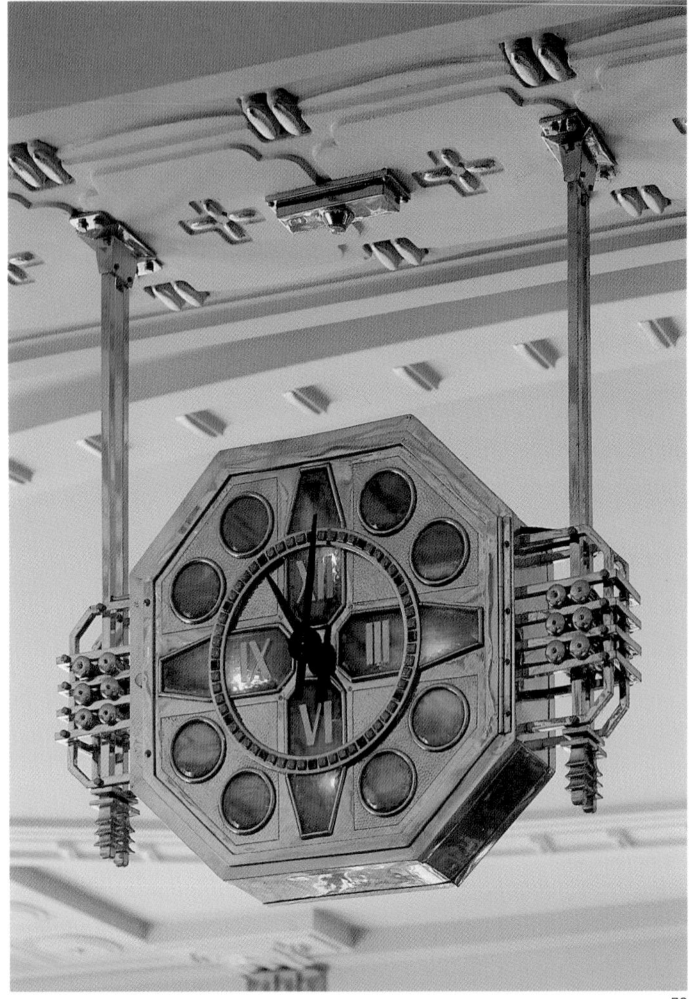

> 78

> 79

78 > Clock above the balcony

79 > Fountain, detail

80 > Booth at the head of the Café and a fountain

> 80

> 81

> 82

81 < Entrance, view of a parlor wall
82 < Entrance to the gallery
83 > Wall with glass panes of the entrance to the gallery
84 > Vestibule

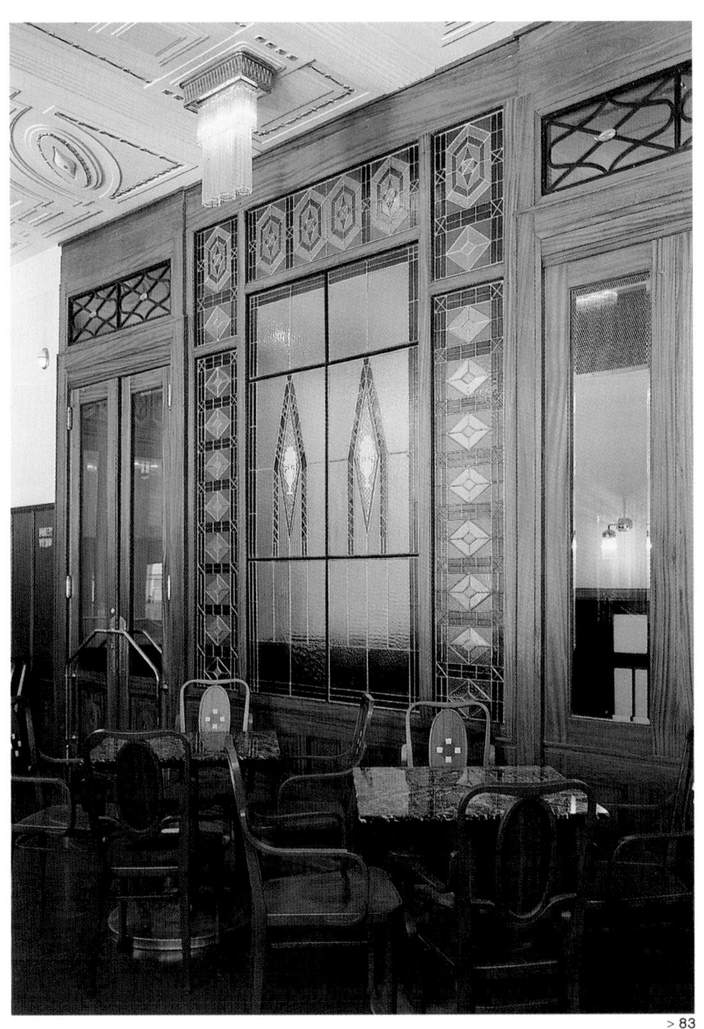

> 83

> 84

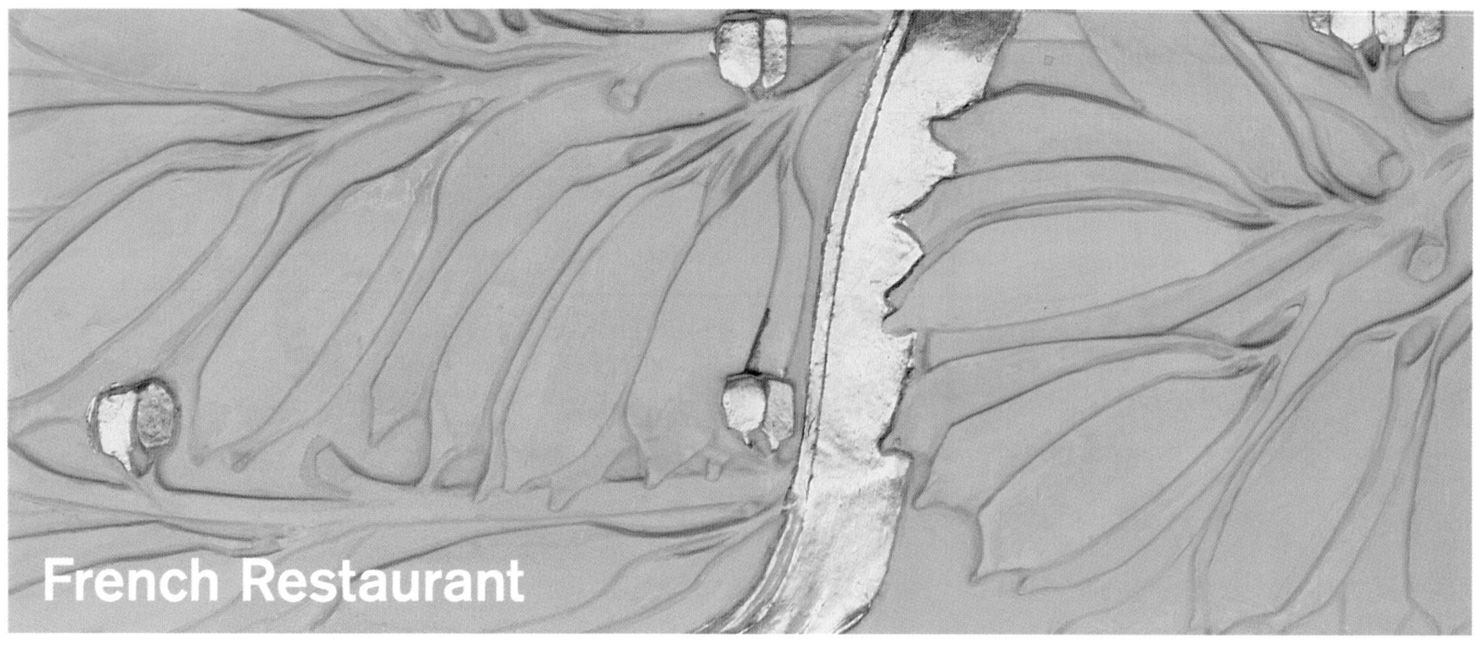

French Restaurant

On the right side of the entrance hall there is a door with elegant glass panels leading into the luxurious French Restaurant, which takes up the whole north wing of the front part of the Municipal House. It is a large rectangular hall with a raised parlor at the head of the room, an oblong side gallery opposite a large "window wall", and a spacious balcony above the main entrance.

The restaurant has seven axes and a flat ceiling. It is quite interesting to note that the rectangular sections of the ceiling, determined by joists, are not harmonized with the pillar grid of the window wall. The ceiling sections are filled with oval centerpieces with stucco decoration of Art-Nouveau female mascarons.

The large windows, similar to those in the Café in the opposite wing, provide "formal" lighting of the restaurant. This is not only because of their size and the articulation of the windows, but also due to the beveled glass panes, which are at places framed in brass frames. The windows are all original, single-leaf windows, and glass screens are placed in front of them in winter. In addition to the rank of side sash windows with unique, built-in chain controls, the room gets a lot of light through the front glass-pane wall of the raised parlor. Despite its similar construction, this large, richly articulated window does not open.

A side gallery with decorative oak railing is situated opposite the rank of windows and between the pillars of the left wall. The gallery is accessible from an inconspicuous wooden horse-shoe shaped staircase which once could be used to descend directly into the Pilsen Restaurant in the basement.

Under the balcony, next to the entrance with beveled mirrors, there are two parlors hidden behind screens and separated by hangings with appliqués.

There is also rich stucco gilded decoration both on the ceiling and the walls of the French Restaurant. The decoration, made by the František Kraumann company, consists mainly of geometrical ornaments complemented by botanical and figural motifs.

On the pillars of the gallery as well as between the sash windows there are mirrors with brass lighting units, harmonized with the huge, highest-quality chandeliers with lusters. The two rows of chandeliers dominate the ceiling and even, thanks to their low suspension, the whole room. When the impressive row of lighting units under the gallery railing is also lit, the value and quality of the lighting stands out. All of the lighting units as well as the ceiling lights in the lower parts and the candelabrum lights on the balcony were supplied by the Prague firm of František Anýž.

A clock, the finest specimen of the quality metalwork in this room, hangs in the passageway into the raised parlor at the front of the restaurant. The clock's rich brass decorative structure is complemented by stylized twigs, glass lusters, lights, and colored glass pieces. Above the clock, under a symbolic relief of a mother with a child, there is a polychrome coat-of-arms of the Old Town of Prague; next to it there are coats-of-arms of the other four historical towns of Prague.

The side segments with vistas into the parlor are at the top decorated with two allegorical murals called "Hop-growing" and "Viniculture" by Josef Wenig. The same author painted a large mural on the side wall called "Prague Receiving her Guests". The solid oak furnishing of the room, as well as the wall wainscoting, partition walls between the booths with upholstered seats, the radiator covers, and cupboards are mostly original and show the perfect craftsmanship of the firm of Ant. Baumgart and Son. Originally, as we know from period photographs, chairs without upholstery were used in the French Restaurant, the same as those used in Sladkovský Hall. To increase the comfort, the chairs used in the restaurant today are upholstered in leather to match the benches in the booths.

Between the central pillars under the gallery, there is a bar with a cupboard decorated with reliefs of Art-Nouveau female half-figures. The top part is embellished with a decorative, stained-glass figural motif of a reclining female figure with stylized floral motifs and two stripes of geometrical ornaments along both sides.

The floor is covered with linoleum of a muted crimson color – as in most halls of the Municipal House. From today's viewpoint, linoleum does not belong among the luxurious attributes of an interior, but at that time, linoleum was an interesting novelty. To preserve the optical originality of the whole interior, linoleum, made according to the original color and

85 << Side wall with a sash window
86 > Josef Wenig, Viniculture

technology, was laid even here, in a luxurious restaurant. For today's visitors and for an increased sense of luxury, it was in places covered with carpet runners.

The raised parlor has a ceiling articulated by intersecting, wide, fluted stripes, with a centerpiece for a chandelier. It is richly adorned with fans of stylized linden twigs and with decorative still-life paintings in oval medallions along the main axes of the perimeter frame. On the walls of the parlor, the original wallpaper is preserved. It was discovered under later layers of paint and restored during the complete reconstruction of the Municipal House. The original furnishing of the parlor, made by the same firm which furnished the restaurant, is complemented by an attached lunette picture called "Hradčany and the New World in Spring" by Adolf Zahel. It was placed in an original frame in 1938 when this painter and restorer was renovating the murals in the French Restaurant. The original damaged lunette painting by Jindřich Tomec called "Prague in the Evening from the West" was then taken down because of its poor condition and stored in the Gallery of the City of Prague. Currently the restored painting is in the side hallway outside the Czech Club.

Also in the gallery and on the balcony, the restaurant's original furnishing, wainscoting, and lighting units were complemented by replicas and new items were added to complete the room.

A door with rich stained-glass panes connects the gallery and a hallway leading to the cloakrooms of the FOK Orchestra. Plaques with the busts of two famous orchestra conductors – Václav Smetáček and Václav Talich – decorate this hallway. There are four other rooms, originally called "Chambers", which used to be furnished like the dining parlors of a middle-class apartment. These rooms served those who, because of their modest living conditions, could not invite a large group of people into their home.

The French Restaurant is typical of prestigious, select, high-quality restaurants in the Prague Art-Nouveau style. With respect to the exterior of the Municipal House, the exceptional character of the French Restaurant is emphasized by decorative lighting units with lusters, which are placed directly in the window reveals, and thus illuminate both its exterior and interior.

> 86

87 > View from the raised parlor near the main entrance

88 >> View from the side gallery of the clock in the passage to the parlor
89 >> Window wall with mirrors

> 88

> 90

> 91

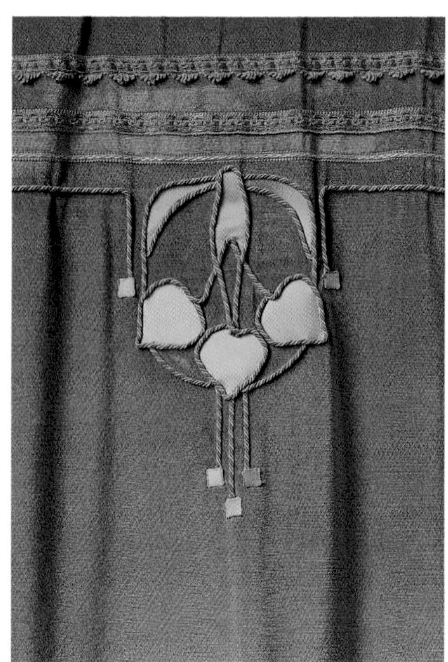

> 92

90 < Hangers in the restaurant's cloakroom
91 < Railing of the stairs leading to the gallery
92 < Door hanging, detail of embroidery
93 > Fitting of an inscription panel
94 > Wooden wainscoting, detail
95 > Stucco decoration

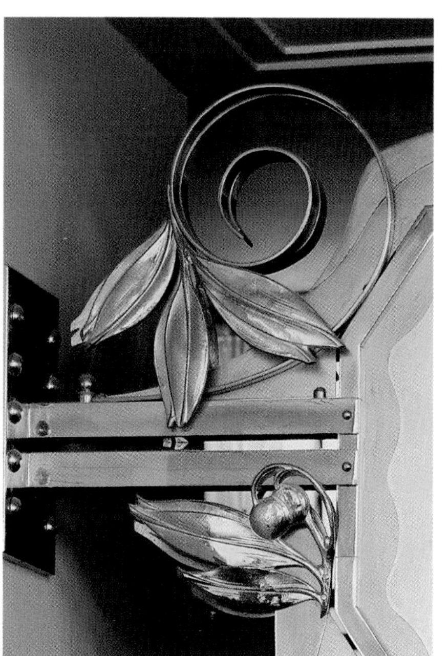

> 93

> 94

> 95

> 96

> 97

96 < View of the restaurant from the raised parlor

97 > Decoration above the passage to the parlor

> 98

98 < View into the parlor at the head of the restaurant

> 99

99 < Restaurant's sash window with a light
100 > Ceiling lights
101 > Standing lamp on the balcony

> 100

> 101

> 102

> 103

> 104

102 < Josef Wenig, Prague Receiving her Guests
103 < Balcony above the entrance
104 > Cupboard with decorative stained glass, behind the bar

105–106 > Stairway to the gallery
107 > View of the restaurant from the side stairway
108 > Vestibule of the restaurant

> 105

> 106

> 107

Basement Foyer

A visitor encounters quite a different atmosphere as soon as he enters the side stairways, leading left and right from the main foyer into the basement. Instead of the palatial, ornate above-ground floors, with excessive gilding and marble, there are ceramic tiles on the walls and granite stairs, all, at first glance, in muted colors. At first sight, this sharp contrast of the humble basement and the decoratively luxurious and above-ground floors that are full of light brings out mixed feelings. However, when an observant visitor gets used to it, he can discover the hidden elegance of the decorative tiles in a program of monumental architecture and decoration. Perfect arts-and-crafts work with the subtlest details is a matter of course. This atmosphere accompanies the visitors in all of the basement rooms, only changing its "color" in accordance with the different halls.

Ceramic slate-blue tiling runs along the stairway walls to the basement level. The tiling is bordered by a black plinth and a finishing black stripe. Relief ceramic pictures, square tiles with stylized flowers, and vertical, colored ornamental bands further articulate the tiling. The wall of the landing, made of muted terrazzo, is decorated with a stucco, patina-coated sculpture of a "Child with a Dog", three side mirrors, and a wooden display case with glass panes on each side.

Two columns on the landing, wainscoted with artificial marble, and with gilded stucco composite capitals, carry the arcades of the stairway shoulders. This is also where a decorative railing running into the basement and ground floor starts.

The main room of the basement foyer forms an entrance hall into the basement restaurants. The hall is divided by six pillars into bays with barrel vaults and lunettes. The bays are separated by arch rings, stretching to the semi-pillars along the perimeter walls. The vault's surface is made of textured finish, combined with smooth moldings that border the lunettes, the arch rings, and the arcade fronts.

In the center of each bay, a newly designed brass lighting unit is fitted. It is tapered, with clear glass and four uncovered bulbs along the perimeter. These lighting units are complemented by four rows of three bulbs in each bay. The walls and pillars are tiled with slate-blue ceramic tiles with inserted black-and-white chessboard stripes. Decorative relief tiles with stylized red beetles are placed among them. The plinth around the hall consists of black ceramic tiles. A black tile band skirts the tiling above a broken line of opalescent squares.

A wall-mounted ceramic fountain with fluted pillars and concave bowl enlivens and adds artistic value to the main wall. The fountain wall is decorated with opalescent tiles arranged in vertical stripes and at the top also with pieces of blue glass. Vistas of old Prague are placed in the ceramic tiling on both sides of the fountain. They were made in the Rakovník fire-clay factory.

The dominating tile floor of the foyer is composed of wavy lines with an engraved spiral décor in terra cotta and beige colors. The tiles are arranged in horizontal stripes with a terra cotta border along the perimeter of the hall, which carries the engraved brand mark of the supplier: "RAKO". This original ceramic floor with a hard and sturdy surface is of the highest quality, which is why it has been preserved in its original state, even on such an exposed place, for almost a century.

PROGRAM

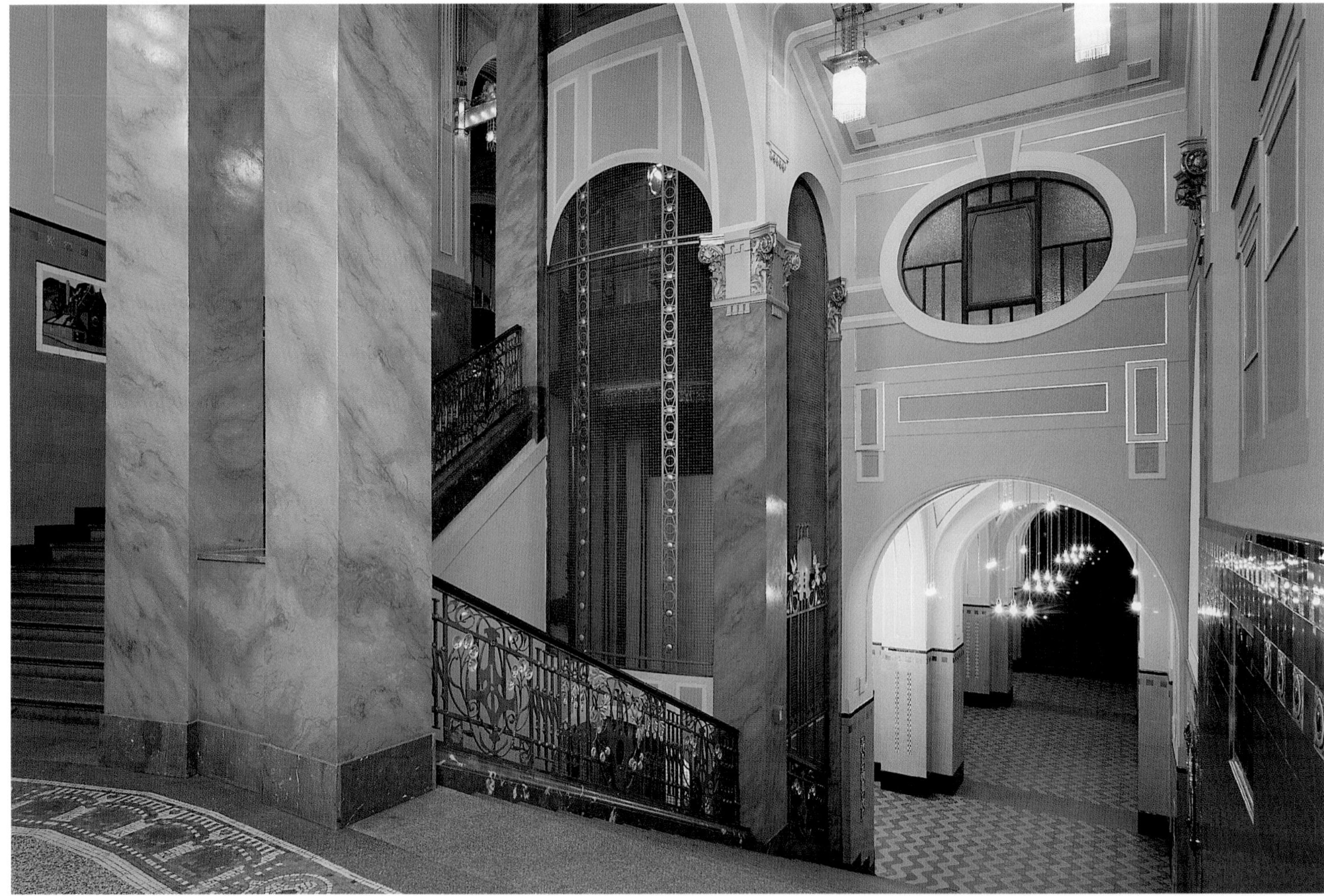

> 110

109 << Stairway landing with a relief by Antonín Mára

110 > Stairway to the basement

111–112 > Ceramic tiling of the stairway to the basement

113 > Relief by Antonín Mára on the landing

> 111

> 112

> 113

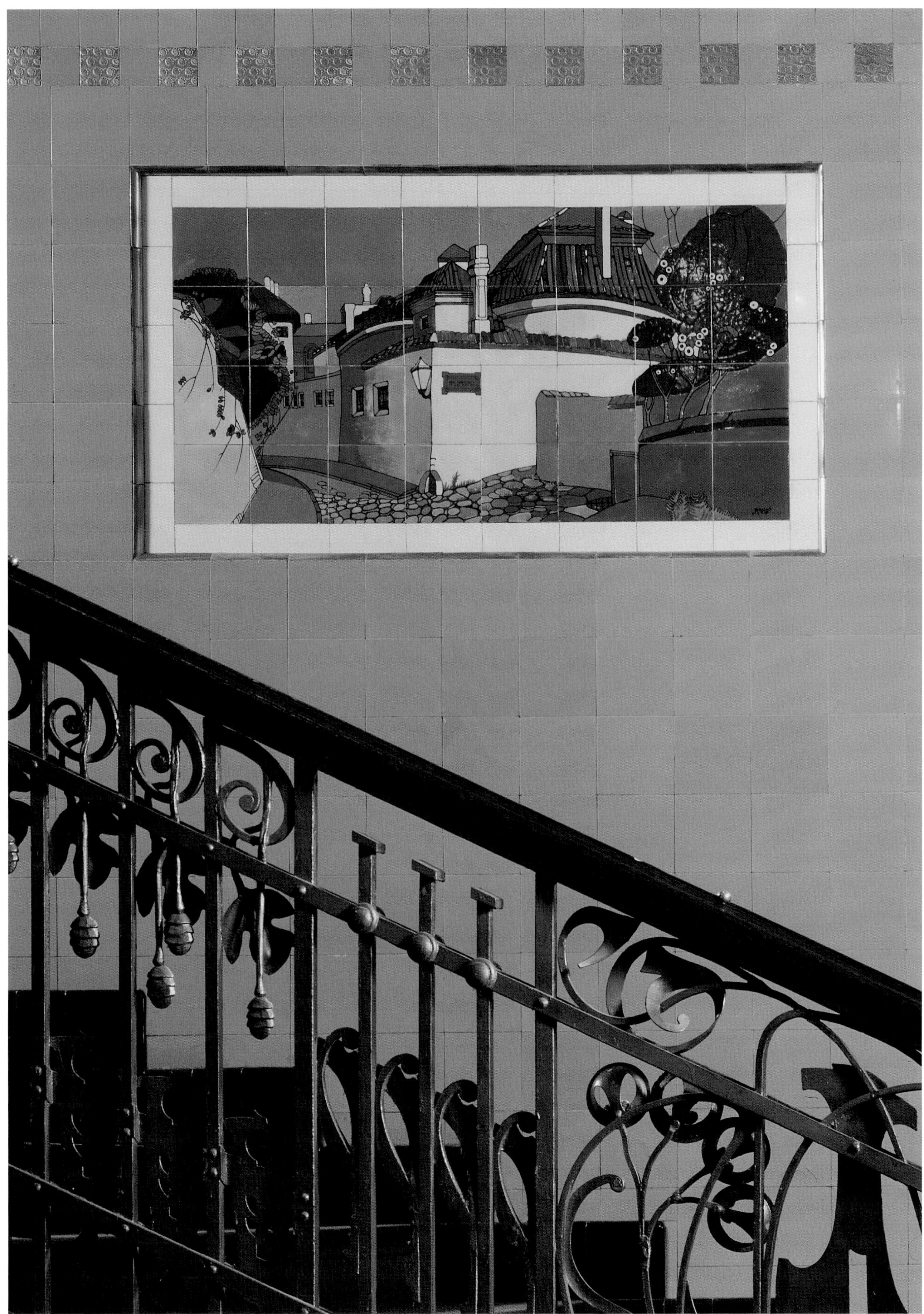

> 114

114 < Ceramic picture of Černínská Street in the New World
115–117 > Details of the ceramic tiling

> 115

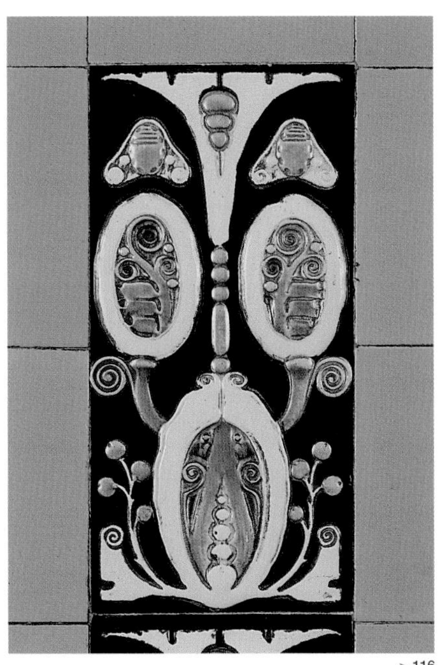

> 116

> 117

> 118

118 < Fountain, detail
119 > Basement foyer lighting
120 > Floor of the foyer

> 119

> 120

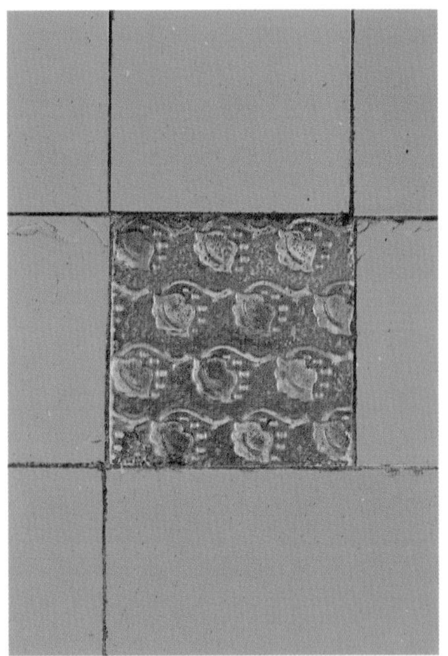

> 121

> 122

121–122 > Details of ceramic tiling
123 > Fountain

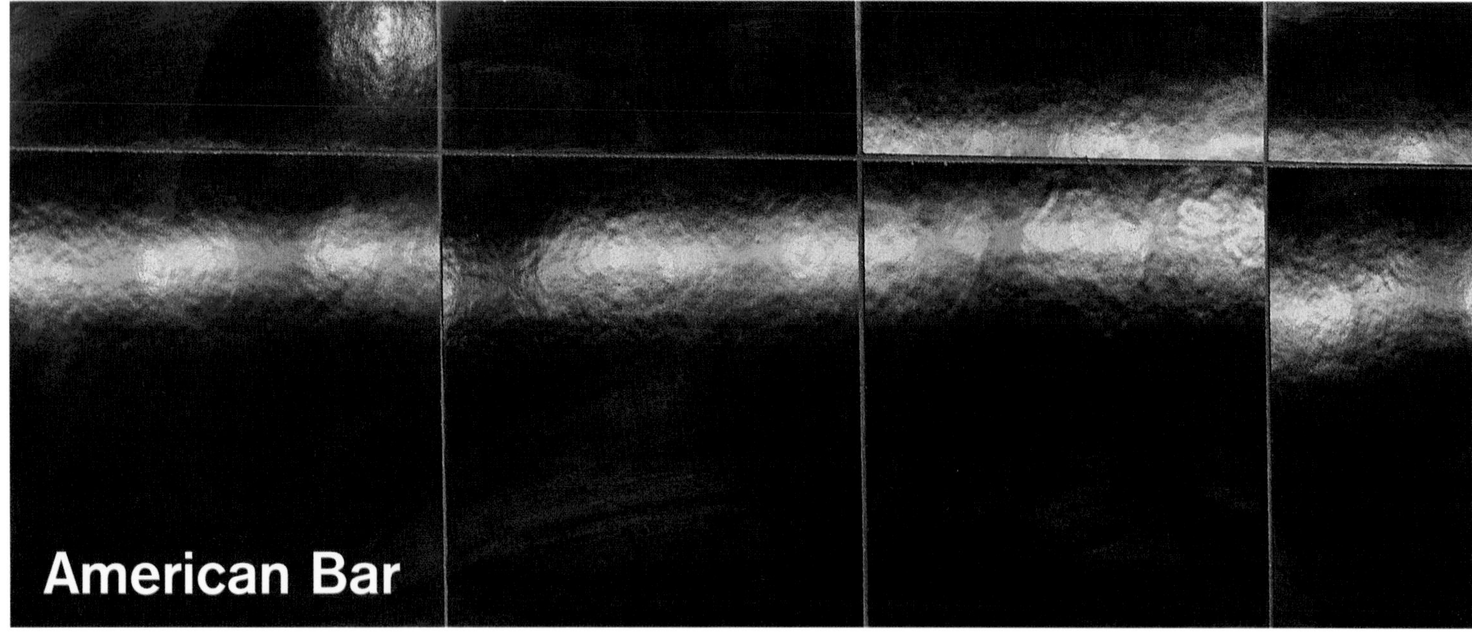

American Bar

To understand the name and the supplemental decoration by American flags, we have to go back to the times of the Municipal House construction – to the beginning of the 20th century. Democracy in the USA and ideas from the New World were at that time a great model and helped to define the patriotic and political ideals of the time of the establishment of the democratic republic. We have to bear in mind that at that time Prague was just a provincial city of the Austro-Hungarian Empire and that the Municipal House was designed to be the site of a thorough presentation of the national culture and history, as well as proof of the versatile abilities, skills, and progressive attitudes of the Czech nation.
The American Bar was probably the first prominent public place in the whole Empire where women were allowed to go to without being accompanied by men. This was a direct consequence of the American Ladies Club, established by Vojtěch Náprstek, where progressive ideas, not only about women's emancipation but also about running a household using modern machines, were developed – it was a place of rich cultural life.
The circular room is prominently located in the central axis of the building. Similarly to all of the privileged rooms, the bar is vaulted by an elliptical dome with thick-bordered lunettes around the room. The vault surface is covered with elongated golden dots to create the feeling that the ceiling is higher than it is.
An artistically unique element of the ceiling is the main chandelier, designed in the shape of a mosaic stained-glass wreath with four jewel-cut boxes. Along the perimeter of each box, there are four suspended glass spheres. The chandelier, supplied by the František Křižík company, is complemented in the center with a drawing with a heron motif by Mikoláš Aleš.
The walls up to the springing line are lined with black ceramic tiling, which on the pillars is decorated with copies of colored drawings by Mikoláš Aleš from 1910–1911. The drawings, fitted in unusual brass frames, represent allegories of different trades: a barrel maker, a countrywoman with geese, a gardener, a butcher, a fisherman with a fish, a beater with a hare.
New wall-mounted lights, made of wrought brass sheets and with lusters, were attached in the vault's springers. These lights were made according to period photographs.
The doors of the main central entrance from the foyer in the basement as well as those of the two side entrances, are large double doors with glass panels and twisted door handles. The lunette fanlights are filled with finely crafted decorative grill, and the perimeter of the archivolt is skirted by a band consisting of beveled mirrors.
Two arcade niches on the sides of the entrance from the vestibule are filled with beveled mirrors and bordered with a band of opalescent ceramic tiles. At the top of the arcade there is a brass grill. The two five-sided niches next to the bar have convergent ribbed panel vaults.
Stepped frames on the walls enclose drawings of pastoral scenery: "At the Hunt", "A Gentleman's Arrival to a Pub", "A Feast in a Pub", "Shrove Tuesday". The stepped frames are harmonized with a stepped plaster design on the walls. The major decoration of the booths is provided by radiator covers of black tiles set in brass frames, with front wrought grill and a top grill attachment with glass panes. The corner booths, furnished with then modern furniture, are concealed behind textile hangings with appliqués.
The ceiling lights are newly added. A new bar, also designed according to period photographs, is made of black marble, with side glass cases, with a back show case with mirrors, and many lusters and side lights. The upholstered benches with two side tables and one round table in front of the mirror walls were also added recently. The floor is covered with new black linoleum.
Despite the "folk-style" decoration with prevailing folk motifs, the accompanying American flags were a logical next step in the perception of the rapid progress of the time. At that time, the flags represented strong symbols of democracy, which was enhanced by the fact that they were placed in a public place of the Austro-Hungarian Empire.

> 124

124 << View from the main entrance

125 > View of the foyer from the American Bar
126 > Bar light

> 125

> 126

> 127

127 < Radiator cover
128 > Mirror wall
129 > Case on a bar with a view of a booth
130 > Seating area

> 128

> 129

> 130

131 > Mikoláš Aleš, A Countrywoman with Geese
132 > Bar stools
133 > View towards the entrance to the Pilsen Restaurant

> 131

> 132

Wine Bar

The floor plan of the "Wine Bar" occupies the basement rooms under the large Café. It has a vault consisting of six bays with oval lunettes, designed to fit the width of the windows and passageways. The bays are separated by wide elliptical stucco molds with gilded dots, which stretch to the pillars attached to the wall. The stucco decoration was made by František Kraumann.

Newly designed, tall lighting units, placed in this hall, were made according to period photographs. The chandeliers have an irreplaceable decorative function because of both their size and their colors. They are composed of four bands merging into a circle; at the bottom they are conic and complemented with bright bulbs and lusters. The wooden wainscoting of the walls was supplied by the Sadílek company. The wainscoting is decorated with unique stripes of relief tiles with the motif of a grapevine. The pillar fronts of the arch rings are skirted by a band of rectangular tiles with stylized botanical motifs; the pillars themselves are lined with tiles with a geometrical heart motif. Above them are new lighting units. The combination of relief ceramic and refined woodwork, all made in bright colors, is unique in composition as well as in craftsmanship. The gaiety of colors is due not only to the wood, which is itself naturally heterogeneous, but also to the differently colored glazing as a result of gradual work on the handmade ceramic elements.

Also, the entryways into the adjacent hallway are accentuated by inserted wooden portals, with carved decorative motifs above the vertical pillars, and by inserted bands of relief tiles. The lintels of the frames with triangular gables are adorned with carved decorative bands, and they are complemented with new textile hangings with appliqués. The design of the main entrance door, from the basement foyer, is similar to the neighboring entrance to the Pilsen Restaurant. It is made of wood with colored stained-glass panes and a semicircular fanlight.

The opposite wall with its semicircular windows adds impressive decoration to the room through the rich, bright-colored, stained-glass panes fitted in lead bands. The wainscoting stretches from under the windows to the front oval recess with a wooden platform, with brass grills set in the front of the podium. The platform portal is decorated with stucco molding with ornamental rectangles and a brass clock situated in the portal's center. The bottom part is bordered by a row of bulbs. The paneling of the curved rear wall of the platform is adorned with subtle inlays.

The surface of the vault is enhanced with stucco diamond-shaped gilded pattern. The main feature of the opposite wall, that is on the other side of the long hall, is the entrance portal of a bar, with side lights set in white artificial marble, complemented with side mirrors. The semicircular pediment is enhanced with a decorative ceramic composition of two monkeys and garlands.

The hall's furnishings – tables and chairs – are newly designed and can be modified, for example, for banquets, as well as for chamber concerts. The floor is covered with modern linoleum.

The side parlor has a barrel vault with lunettes. The wainscoted walls are enhanced by original inlaid bands of ceramic tiles and by mirrors. The semicircular fanlight of the partition wall is filled with stained-glass panes in a grill. A phone booth is cleverly inserted into the wainscoting of the side room. Next to it, there is a cupboard and the beginning of the stairway leading to the Café.

The staircase connects the rear of the Wine Bar with the Café, and thus it is very useful when balls and other events take place in the Municipal House, during which various halls are used simultaneously. A similar stairway in the other wing connects the French Restaurant and the Pilsen Restaurant. When the centrally located American Bar is also opened, visitors can enjoy the attractiveness of this interestingly shaped ceremonial area.

> 134

134 << Arcades and passages

> 135

> 136

> 137

135–40 > Lights

141 > A view toward the platform with an arrangement of chairs for a chamber concert

> 138

> 139

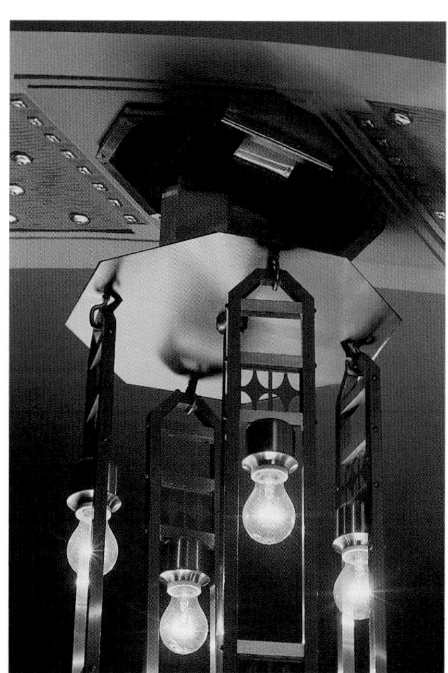

> 140

> 142

142 < Wainscoting of the pillars between the windows

143–145 > Ceramic tiling, details

> 143

> 144

> 145

> 146

> 147

> 148

> 149

146 < Platform
147 < Decorative stained-glass window
148 < Vista from a side parlor
149 < Entrance into the American Bar flanked with lights,
a relief of Monkeys around a Barrel in the door head
150 > Wooden and ceramic wainscoting near the platform
151 > Railing of the stairway leading to the Café

> 150

> 151

> 152

> 153

> 154

152 < Inlaid wooden wainscoting
153 < Air vent grill, detail
154 < Stucco decoration above the platform
155 > Inlaid wooden wainscoting near the platform
156–157 > Wooden wainscoting, details

> 155

> 156

> 157

158 >> Chandelier and a window wall
159 >> Sculpted decoration of the platform niche
160 >> Separating grill, detail
161 >> Monkeys around a Barrel, a relief in the door head leading into the American Bar
162 >> The entrance door from the foyer

> 158

> 159

> 160

> 161

> 162

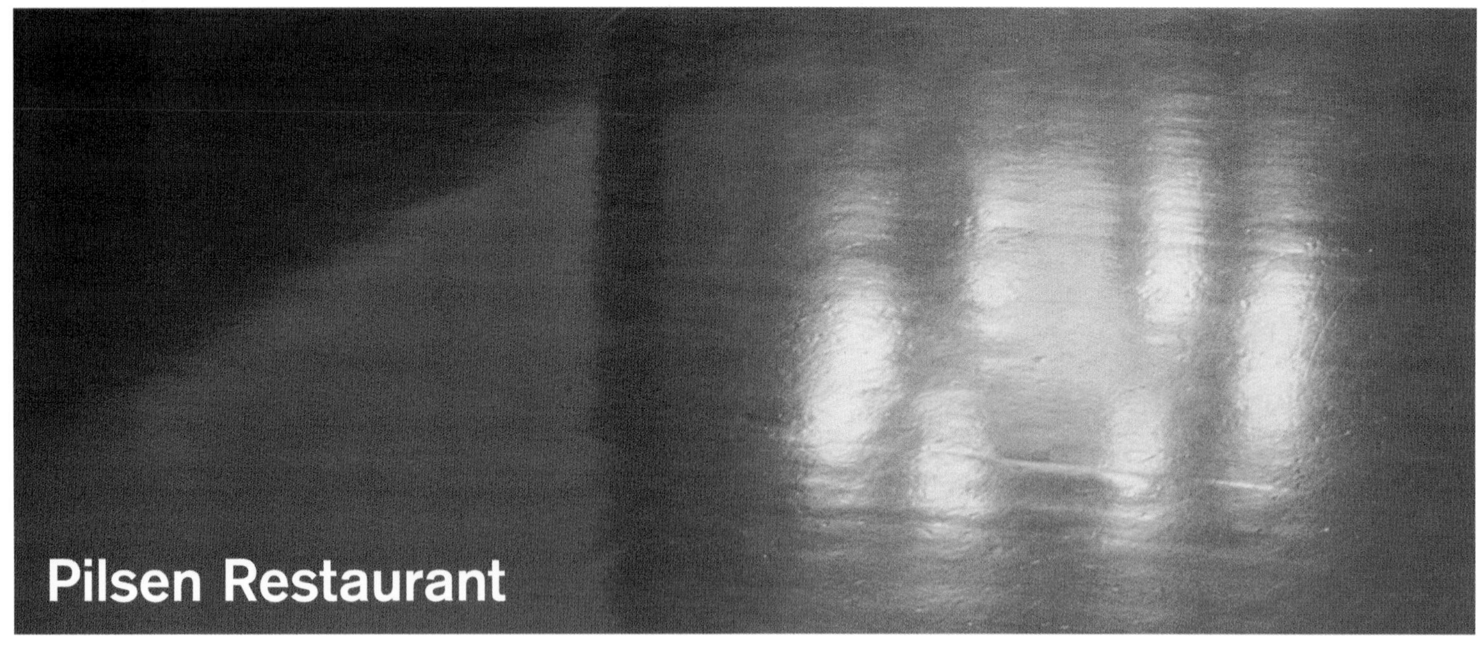

Pilsen Restaurant

The restaurant was originally named "Folk Restaurant", which more accurately captures the designer's intention to create a large brasserie of a folk type with motifs from the Slavonic countryside.

The oblong, vaulted "cellar" space of the Pilsen restaurant, with a raised platform in the front, is characterized by a barrel vault with oval lunettes. The arch rings meet at the top of the lunettes in a running stucco band decorated by layered rectangles. The chandelier structures were designed according to preserved photographs. Four brass poles carry an octagonal frame that is attached to the load-bearing structure by chains, which are supposed to evoke farm barns. The lights hanging down from the frame are complemented in the main axis by an octagonal lantern with a semi-spherical glass cover. The areaways are also an important source of light, "hidden" behind semicircular windows with colored stained glass in lead bands. The yellow hues of the window panes give the impression that the hall is permanently lighted by electric light. The bottom part of the walls is lined with wood wainscoting enhanced with engraved, rustic, colored ornaments. The same wainscoting can be found also on the partition walls of the booths, which make the hall seem larger despite the fact that they clash with the need for an open hall for possible staged folk productions. The booths, however, give the large hall the feeling of coziness and help to evoke a "domestic" country atmosphere.

Dominant colored ceramic tiling starts above the wooden wainscoting and the furniture with colored folk ornaments. The tiles above the wood are of blue hues. At the springing line they are bordered with a colored relief decorative band with the motifs of leaves and fruit. Here, at the springing line, brightly polychrome coats-of-arms of Czech cities decorate the walls.

Both passages into the side rooms are flanked by decorative tile bands. The upper parts of the arches are filled with brass wrought grills, which make a counterpart to the stained-glass semcircular windows. The wall of the passage leading to the bar is decorated by a ceramic mural by Jakub Obrovský, made in Rakovník ceramic. The picture's theme is "Czech harvest" and it covers almost all of the arched wall in tiles of surprisingly bright colors, enlivening the whole room of the restaurant.

The archivolt of the arched entrance is flanked by a decorative band and the head is filled with an ornate wrought grill. The entrance swinging door has stained-glass panes and twisted door handles. The main wall opens into a parlor with a platform and five steps. The top of the arcade's basket arch is decorated with a large polychrome coat-of-arms of the city of Prague, under which hangs an ornamental brass clock. It was newly designed, based on preserved photographs.

The rear wall of the platform is wainscoted, with colored carved motifs, and a built-in bench under the window. A stained-glass window with a motif of cats is an original ornament of the platform. It particularly stands out when looking at the main wall. The chandeliers were newly designed according to period photographs. A part of the adjoining arcade is decorated by two murals, "Boy" and "Girl", and in the ceramic tiling of the wall there are three-side niches with Art-Nouveau urns. Similar, large urns of an unusual red color, placed on the pedestals of the pillars between the windows, can be found alongside the entire hall.

The original furniture, made by the Sadílek company, was supplemented with replicas, including tables and chairs. The number of the original brass free-standing coat racks was also increased. Another striking item is an original refrigerator, which used to be filled with blocks of ice as its source of cold.

The Pilsen Restaurant is the only of the Municipal House halls that does not have a cloakroom. The visitors put their coats by their chairs and benches, which undoubtedly emphasizes the restaurant's folk orientation.

164 > Coat hanger
165 > Ceramic urn in a niche in the front of the restaurant
166 > View of the window wall

> 164

> 165

> 166

167 < View of a parlor in the front of the restaurant. On the walls next to the passage, ceramic pictures of a Boy and a Girl by Jakub Obrovský.

> 168

> 169

168–171 < Ceramic tiling with the coats-of-arms of Czech cities

172 >> Front wall with a ceramic picture by Jakub Obrovský called Czech Harvest

> 170

> 171

> 172

> 173

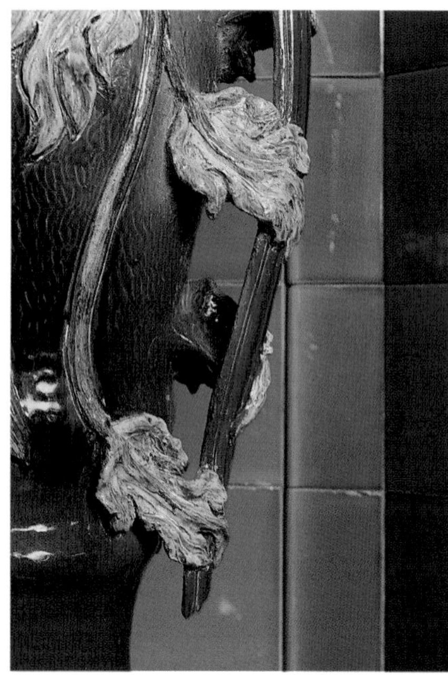
> 174

> 175

173 < The back of the clock in the passage to the raised platform

174–178 > Decoration details

> 176

> 177

> 178

> 179

179 < View towards the entrance to the American Bar

180 > View towards the raised parlor at the head of the restaurant

> 180

181 > Railing of the stairway into the French Restaurant
182 > Wooden wainscoting and chairs
183 > Main entrance from the basement foyer

> 181

> 182

Main Stairway

Adjoining the main hall is a spacious, monumental, triple-aisle hall that allows easy access to all halls and parlors on the top floors of the building as well as entrance into the Central Cloakroom in the mezzanine. The entrance to the basement, independent of the opening to the top floors, is allowed by refined and yet inconspicuously located stairways on the sides of the hall.

After the reconstruction in 1997, a new, somewhat indistinct entrance was added, which leads into a relatively spacious, modern information center and a shop, where gifts and printed materials connected to the Municipal House are sold.

A wide marble stairway is situated in the axis central to the entrance hall and is bordered by marble balustrades and monumental columns. The palatial, luxurious appearance is certainly accentuated also by red runners attached by brass rods with original fittings.

The floor is tiled with high quality terrazzo, with colored borders, articulated by inlaid mosaic ornament. From this main level, the two previously mentioned entrances to side stairways leading to the basement can be approached. They are accentuated by richly ornate structures bearing the names of the basement restaurants and hanging from the ceiling. Their impressive execution in colored stained-glass panes corresponds with the luxury of the whole central entrance hall.

Along the outer sides of the main stairway, pillars, wainscoted with artificial marble with gilded stucco decorations, "frame" the entrances into both ceremonial elevators, mayor's and president's – originally emperor's. The elevator interiors are original; the richly decorated elevator cars were made by the Ringhoffer company.

Opulently decorated booths of the box-office and the reception, located on the sides of the main entrance glass wall adjoining the entrance hall, were also preserved. The names of both booths are eye-catching, especially with their colored stained-glass panes.

The ceiling of the hall, articulated into several rectangular bays, is symbolically supported by stucco female half-figures with horns of plenty. These large sculptures with bronze patina coating as well as other stucco ornaments were made by Jindřich Čapek.

The arcades, made of artificial marble, open to the elevator shafts, are adorned with richly ornate lighting units with glass lusters. Both they and the original sets of lighting units on the ceiling of the hall were made by the František Křižík company.

Both marble stairways continue from the landing outside the Central Cloakroom to the first floor. They are magnificently decorated with both artificial and natural marble. Thanks to the extraordinary quality of the artificial marble, it is hard to distinguish between them at first sight.

The windows with decorative stained glass used to open into a light well that has now been walled in. The elevator shafts are covered with richly adorned, gilded grills with lattices and stylized leaves. The original equipment of the hall includes also notice-board boxes for programs.

The hall landing opens towards the Central Cloakroom by a triple passage with colored stained glass and a clock. The passages can be closed by rolling grate. The landing is at the same time the main connecting space linking the main stairway with both side stairways leading to the first floor and the main halls of the building.

> 184

184 << Vista into the stairway mirror

185 > Side aisle of the stairway hall outside an elevator door
186 > Lighted stained-glass entrance above the entrance into the basement
187 > Box-office booth

> 185

> 186

POKLADNA

188 > Terrazzo floor

189 > Detail of lighted stained-glass inscription panel

190 > Column base and detail of stairs

191 > View of the entrance to the Central Cloakroom

> 188

> 189

> 190

> 192

192 < Light above the main stairway

193 > Lighting above a mirror outside the Central Cloakroom

194 > Elevator doorway decoration and lighted stained glass

> 193

> 194

> 195

> 196

> 197

195 200 < Details of the elevator shaft grills and railings

> 198

> 199

> 200

> 201

> 202

> 203

> 204

201 < Lattice above the elevator doorway with a lighting unit

202–204 > Elevator cabin interior

> 205

> 206

205 < View of the stairway hall

206 > Mascaron in the voussoir of an elevator shaft in the main starway

> 207

> 208

207 < Stairway hall with figural decoration by Jindřich Čapek

208 > Landing outside the Central Cloakroom

Central Cloakroom

The large hall of the "Central Cloakroom" is divided by two rows of eight square columns into three aisles, which are expanded by rounded ridges along both sides of the hall. The distribution of girders corresponds to the main load-bearing structures. These ferroconcrete girders serve as a sturdy means of support for the floor of the largest hall of the building – Smetana Concert Hall.

The Central Cloakroom figures in the extensive, irregular, and multipurpose activities of the Municipal House as a natural piazetta, an inner square, from which all "paths" into halls, clubs, gaming rooms, and restaurants spring. When it was built, this function was even more obvious since it would provide a room where people from different social levels would meet frequently. The visitors to this ceremonial building were heterogeneous just like the possibilities and level of the use and activities of the building. The highest officials of the monarchy, Prague councilors, prominent industrialists as well as workers, representatives of avant-garde culture, and ordinary citizens could all meet here at the same time – some while attending social events, others while visiting a club or a meeting while their wives would enjoy themselves in the Confectionery or in the American Bar, some coming to see an exhibition or a concert, and others coming to a restaurant or renting a dining parlor. Simply, the Municipal House made the extraordinary possible: heterogeneous, 24-hour use by a diverse public, which before the independent republic was established had only been tied together by growing patriotism. This actually fulfilled the original idea of establishing such a unique building. That is why the Central Cloakroom plays such an irreplaceable role. Adequate to this role is not only its spaciousness but also its furnishing with comfortable benches, and at one time even a separate box for expensive coats and fur coats, which could be hung by the ceiling.

The walls of this efficiently and clearly arranged cloakroom, with original metal coat-rack structures, are covered in textured wallpaper in a muted gray color. The pillars and walls are decorated with mirrors, above which nickel sconces are attached, newly made according to historical documentation. The same surfacing is also on the new chandeliers and lighting units, hanging in rows from the girders. The floor is now covered by terrazzo; however, originally there were hexagonal whitish ceramic tiles. The cloakroom capacity was reduced during the reconstruction of the Municipal House; the counters were not made according to the original scope. Originally, the cloakroom was designed for maximum simultaneous use of all halls.

The original plans presumed that the cloakroom would be also used by the performers, especially the choir members. In the present day, they, as well as the orchestra members and soloists, have different rooms in other parts of the building at their disposal. The original booths for ladies to fix their hair were also removed.

The windows with ornamental panes used to open into the light well. Today, after its cancellation, the room is artificially lighted. At the back of the Central Cloakroom, new benches and mirrors were added. To increase the safety of the people gathered in one hall, the original accesses to the restrooms by two wooden side staircases were lowered to the level of the main floor.

New passages at the back of the cloakroom enable stair access to the new foyer with the information center, as well as to the new rehearsal room under the stage of Smetana Hall.

II
235-352

> 210

210 < Lighting units above the mirrors on the pillars, and on the ceiling girders
211–212 > Hangers, details

213 >> Vista from a side entrance

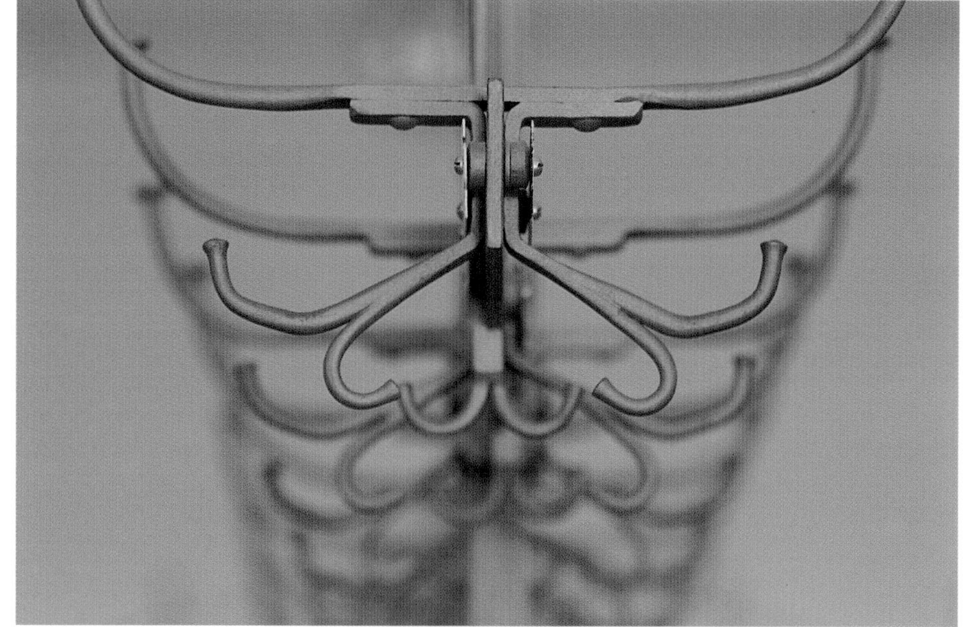
> 211

> 212

214–215 > Wall fittings
216 > Chandelier
217 > Diagonal view of the Central Cloakroom

> 214

> 215

> 216

The Billiard and Gaming Rooms

The mezzanine is accessible by an independent entrance from a side stairway, through a swinging door with a brass grill incorporated into a glass wall. The fanlight is adorned with stained glass. However, on the other side, the gaming rooms can be, if needed, directly connected to the Café. This is not only to provide refreshment, but by connecting these two spaces, all of the billiard and gaming rooms and the Café can be operated together.

A part of the main hallway is on the left side extended into a semicircular niche with a round table and a banquette. They, together with a decorative mosaic band in polychrome stucco on the wall, make for a very cosy nook. On the right side, the hallway opens with a triple arcade into the billiard room. Below the stained-glass fanlight, an ornate set of cabinets is built into the entrance. The opposite wall is covered with mirrors, with two cabinets jutting out from the wainscoting. The hallway is completed by a cupboard with stained-glass panes and two radiator covers with marble panels. All is complemented with mirrors and wall fittings.

The billiard room walls are wainscoted in wood and house built-in radiator covers with marble surfaces. A row of banquettes sits under the windows. An eye-catching element on the front wall is a wooden panel with two mirrors and a clock between brass grills. The arcade pillars are covered with an inlaid wooden case for billiard cues and built-in abacuses for scorekeeping. Ceiling lights of wrought brass sheets with bulbs hang above them.

The room is furnished with new pool tables, above which new brass banks of lights are hung. Each bank contains nine glass cones which ensure uniform lighting of the pool tables. Everything was newly made, based on period photographs. The next room was designed as a master billiard parlor in the same style.

The most striking feature of the wainscoting in the wedge-shaped passage, which leads to the card parlor, is a column with a brass clock. The wall adjoining the hallway is completed by built-in cabinets with stained-glass panes in the fanlight.

The framed panels of the walls are filled with wallpaper. Under the ceiling, a decorative sculpted molding stretches around the whole room. Unusual brass chandeliers with cascading glass lusters hang from the ceiling, decorated with stucco rectangular bands. The parlor is furnished with card tables and chairs with inlaid back rests, recreated according to period photographs.

The billiard and gaming rooms were restored to the original form from the beginning of the 20th century, despite the fact that today's equipment and function of gaming rooms – as generally understood – reaches to gambling machines and casinos.

To use the rooms more efficiently, especially the elongated room with the row of pool tables, the interior can be temporarily equipped with exhibition tables for showing small objects and graphic art.

> 218

219 < View from a wedge-shaped parlor into the room with the master pool table

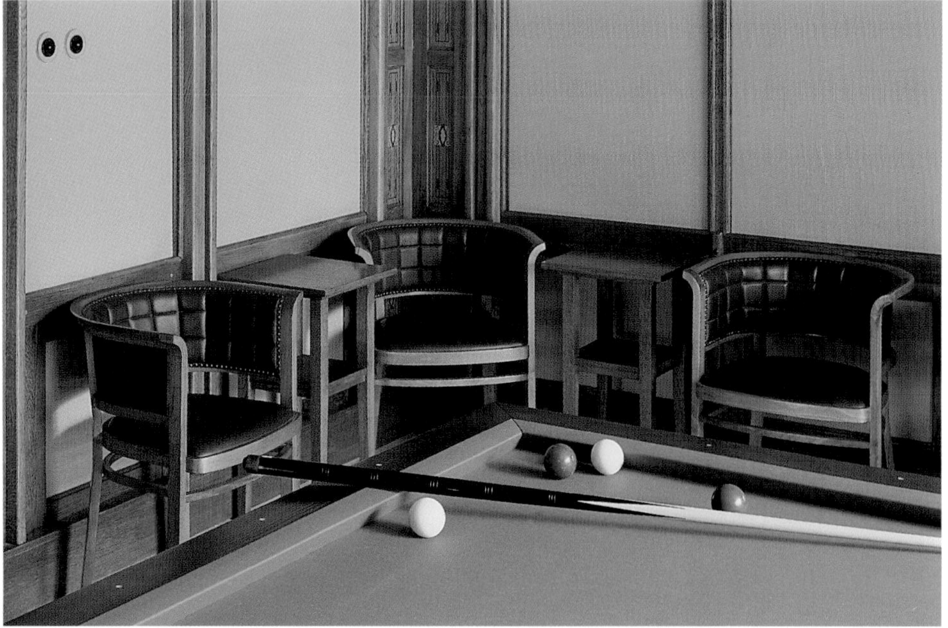

> 220

220 > Equipment of a master billiard room

221 > Abacus with a bell by the master pool table

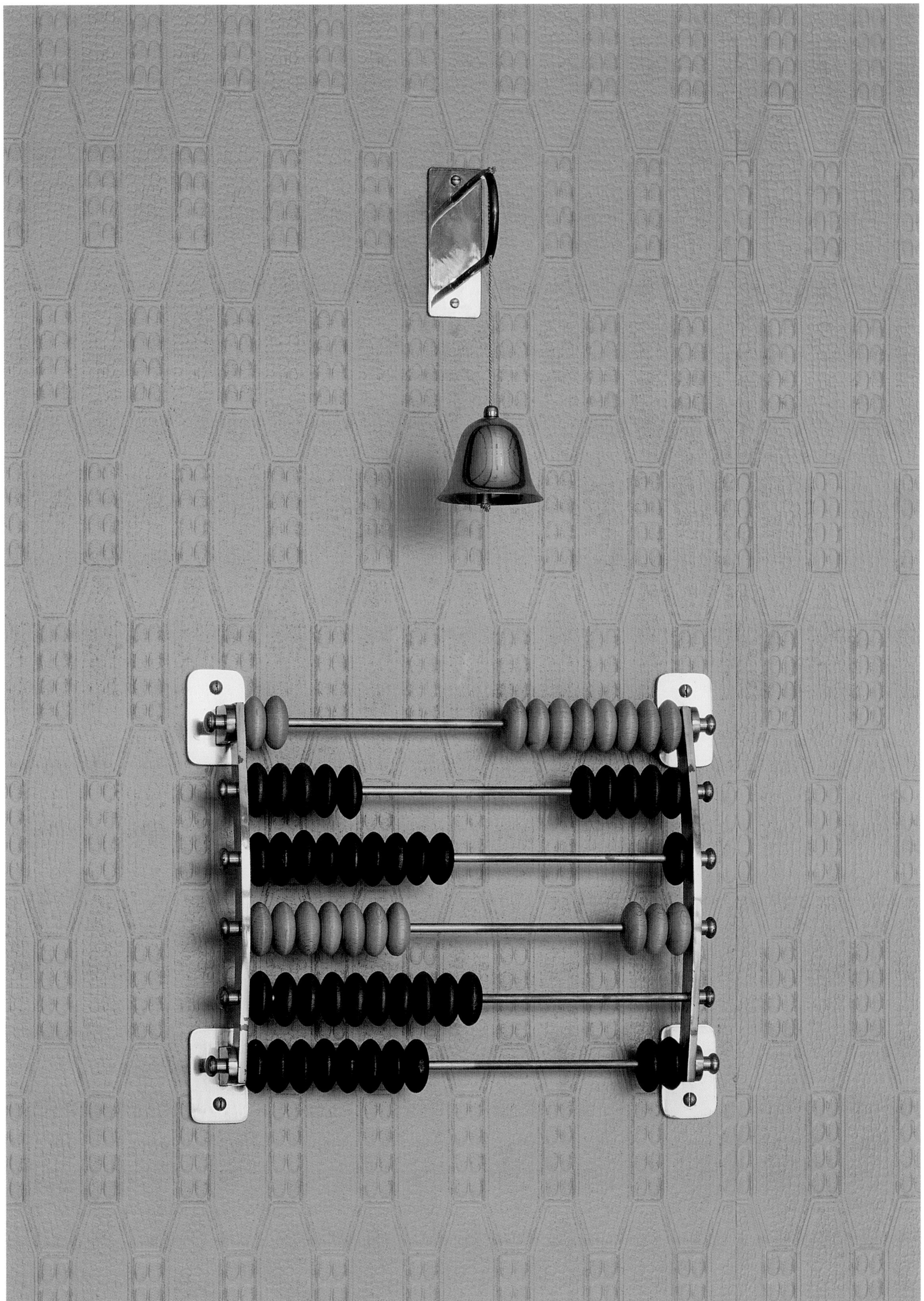

> 222

222 << Billiard room

223–224 > Inlays, detail

225 > Mirror wall at the head of a billiard room

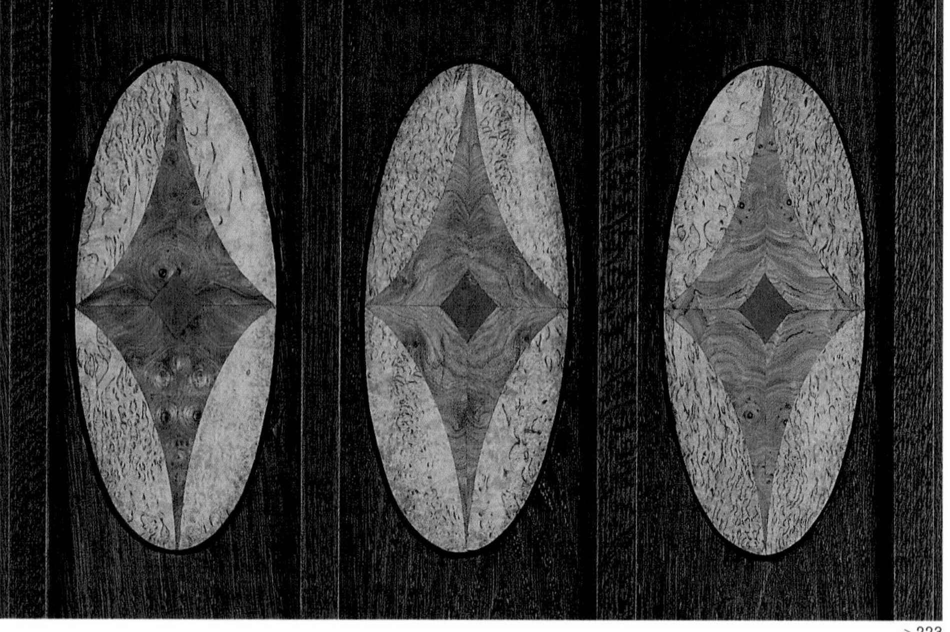

> 223

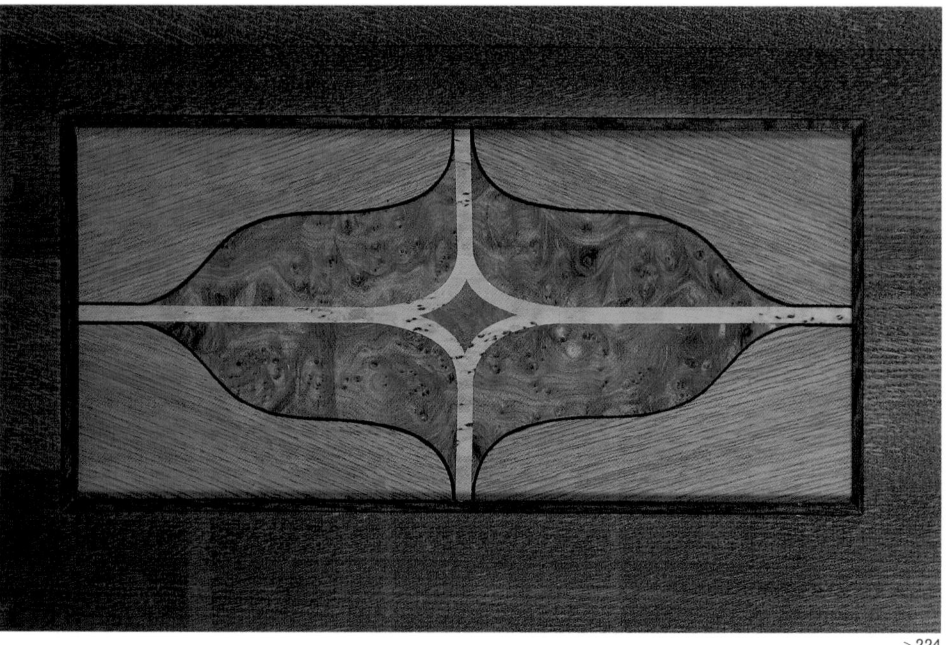

> 224

> 226

> 227

226 << Billiard room with a master pool table

227 < Wall fitting
228–230 > Lights

> 228

> 229

> 230

> 231

> 232

> 233

231–233 < Lights
234 > Mirror light in the corridor
235 > Wall fitting in a billiard room
236 > Detail of a lighting unit above a pool table

237 >> Lighting unit above a pool table
238 >> Chandelier in the card room

> 234

> 235

> 236

> 237

> 238

239 > Passage between billiard rooms

240 > Card room equipment
241 > Back of an armchair in the card room
242 > Card room

> 240

> 241

> 242

> 243

> 244

> 245

243 << Window wall in the card room
244 << View of a billiard room from a corridor

245 < View of a niche with a table and a banquette from a billiard room
246–247 > Wedge-shaped parlor outside a billiard room
248 > Detail of a billiard room equipment

> 246

> 247

> 248

249 > Mosaic in the niche of the gaming-rooms corridor
250 > Ceramic tiling outside the entrance into the gaming rooms
251 > Corridor outside the gaming parlors, detail

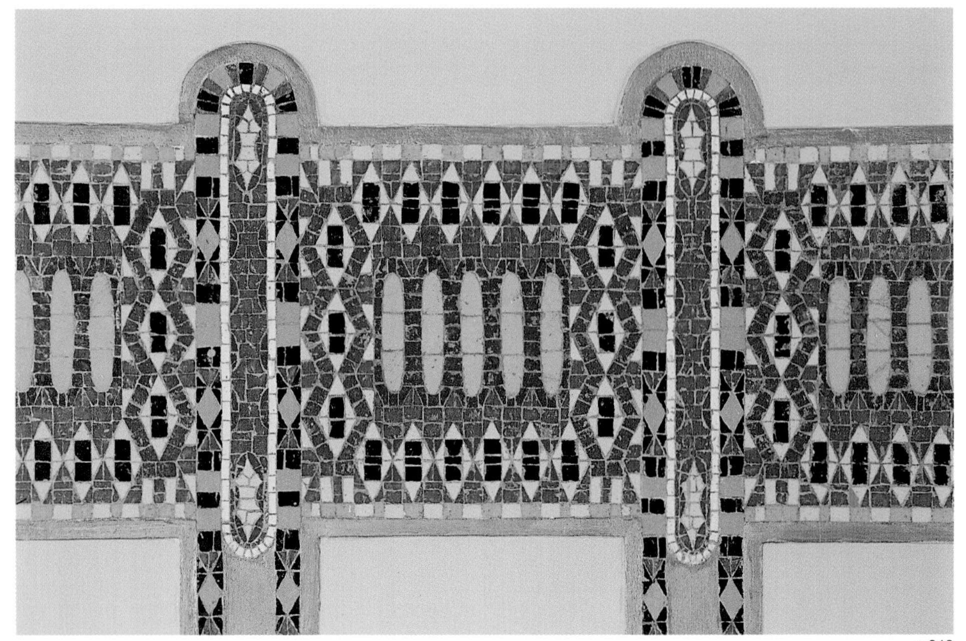
> 249

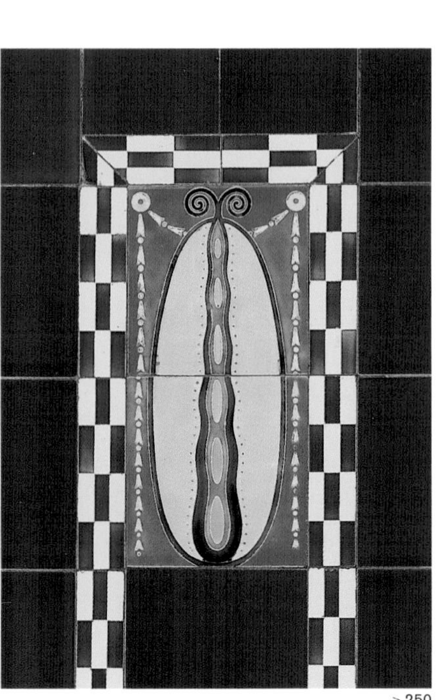
> 250

First-Floor Foyer and Corridors

The main foyer connects the various elements of the first-floor plan. It is designed symmetrically around the central axis of the entrances into Smetana Hall and the Mayor's Hall. Both sides of the foyer contain luxurious stairway shoulders and loan the hall the air of a palace.

Along the perimeter, the foyer is articulated by square pillars, semi-columns, and pilasters. To the east, it is open to the corridor outside the ceremonial parlors of the front bay. The walls, as well as the vertical elements, are wainscoted with artificial marble of brown, white, and terra cotta colors. Pillars and pilasters have low plinths with Tuscan bases and Art-Nouveau gilded composite capitals. The artfully accentuated fronts of the elevator shafts between the inner pilasters of the staircase make a portal composition with a pair of pilasters with fluted capitals and circular disks. Situated above the lintel is a decorative sopraporta of a classicizing form with a naturalistic garland, crested with an oval medallion of the profile of a head. The detail work is carried out in dark patina-coated, gilded plaster.

The jamb of the elevator entrance is made of white artificial marble into which a double elevator door is set. The door is composed of beveled glass panes set in brass frames. The pilasters around the elevator shaft carry brass two-arm sconces with lusters.

The ceiling with centerpieces is architecturally very impressive. Its lunettes are designed to concur with the width of the arcades. The high cove is in spandrels decorated with Art-Nouveau cartouches with linden leaves and by the centerpieces it is emphasized by textured plaster. The ceiling segment consists of three parts, defined by supporting beams with linear molded soffits and cornices around the inner perimeter. The center is accentuated by a rectangular frame with a groined centerpiece with small rectangles along the perimeter. The side bays are adorned with corrugated stucco areas of irregular shapes, set in sculpted segments with rich Art-Nouveau stucco botanical decoration.

The large, cascading ceiling chandeliers with glass lusters are completed by four rows of seven bulbs with cylindrical covers. The structure of the entrance oak wall with glass panels, leading into Smetana Hall, is decorated with carved botanical motifs, emblems, and eye-catching geometrical brass door handles. It is a more elaborate variant of the ground-floor entrance door. The door's stained-glass decoration consists of beveled and diamond-cut glass, also set in brass frames. A brass clock is situated in the central band of the delicately composed stained-glass fanlight.

The floor of this luxurious foyer is covered by "ordinary" crimson linoleum. We should pause here to remind ourselves of the specific character of linoleum and its functional features at the time of the building's construction. The building was intended to be multipurpose, a place where many "noisy" activities would take place at the same time. The individual halls are sufficiently separated by hallways, ensuring sound insulation to some extent, but the hallways had to be designed in such a way that the visitors moving from place to place would not disturb a concert, or a conference or meetings in parlors. That is why the period's novelty – linoleum, a material that can suppress the noise of footsteps, is easily maintained, and is impressively shiny when polished – was used. At the time it was an uncommon, but modern, material which was applied on a large scale only in Hofburg in Vienna, and a series of other palaces in Central Europe. This helps to explain why linoleum was used as a complement to the marble wainscoting and gilded stucco decoration in these ceremonial halls.

Adjacent to the central foyer, opposite the entrance to Smetana Hall, runs a section of the east corridor that is articulated by arch rings into three sections with groined vault. The vault surface juxtaposes the coarse textured plaster with the smooth, stucco centerpieces. The ceiling fixtures with lusters are completed by four bulbs. The artificial marble of slate color makes rectangular frames on the terra cotta-colored walls and illusory three-dimensional rectangles along the base of the wall.

In the axis of the foyer as well as this part of the corridor, the entrance to a very important hall of the building – the Mayor's Hall – is artfully formed. A sculpted portal, also made of the artificial marble, decorated by wreaths of patina-coated and gilded stucco, carries a sopraporta with the name of the hall. The top is ornate with a multi-colored coat-of-arms of

SÁL
PRIMATORSKÝ

252 << View of the Mayor's Hall from the foyer

the city of Prague with two sitting male figures with drapery and garlands with ribbons.

The right corridor has a barrel vault articulated into bays by fluted arch rings. Between the rings the wall is decorated with a rich stucco stripe with gilded details of nature motifs. The front wall of the hallway is dominated by a portal with a figural sculpture of two putti with a wreath and linden twigs. A wooden, semicircular window, looking into the mezzanine, completes the wall above the portal.

Above the wall to the former serving room with frosted-glass panes, a mezzanine landing with decorative, typically Art-Nouveau brass railing is projected in segments. The ceiling fixtures are anchored in brass panels. Composed of semi-spherical covers and four bulbs in the corners, they maintain a constant, low level of light, corresponding to the connecting purpose of the hallway.

A series of entrances divide the right wall into parlors. The wall is made of dark oak and has a pediment with a cartouche medallion of a decorative carved female figure in its center. The door wings are paneled with beveled glass panes set in brass frames. Two mirrors with three-part sconces with lusters are attached to the wall. In the lower part, brass plinths for potted flowers are situated. The floral decoration of even the less important halls of important buildings used to be a matter of course and so, the architecture of the period made proper room for it. The wall is completed with a marble panel bearing the inscription of "SLADKOVSKÝ HALL".

The left corridor has a barrel vault with arch rings that softly stretch to the pilaster capitals with botanical motifs. In the center of the bays hang two chandeliers with cascading crystal chains and lusters. The hallway, from the turn towards the Confectionery, is divided by a portal made of artificial marble decorated with a garland with a ribbon.

On the right side of the hallway, similar to the north corridor, the entrance to the former serving room is made in the form of a wooden wall with frosted-glass panes. A segmented mezzanine balcony, with striking, ornamental Art-Nouveau brass railing, arches above this entrance for the personnel.

Two doors that lead into another hall dominate the left wall. They are flanked with striking jambs and are decorated with finely crafted carved rectangles and relief cylinders. The pediment above the door is filled with a white marbel panel with the inscription of "DR. JUL. GRÉGR HALL".

The connecting space is completed by two beveled mirrors and brass plinths for potted flowers. One of the mirrors, set in a wooden frame, is a three-part mirror, vertically articulated in the top extension piece; the second one is set in brass frame with side shelves. An octagonal mirror in a stucco frame is placed under the ceiling.

253 > Soproporta with the coat-of-arms of Prague

> 253

> 254

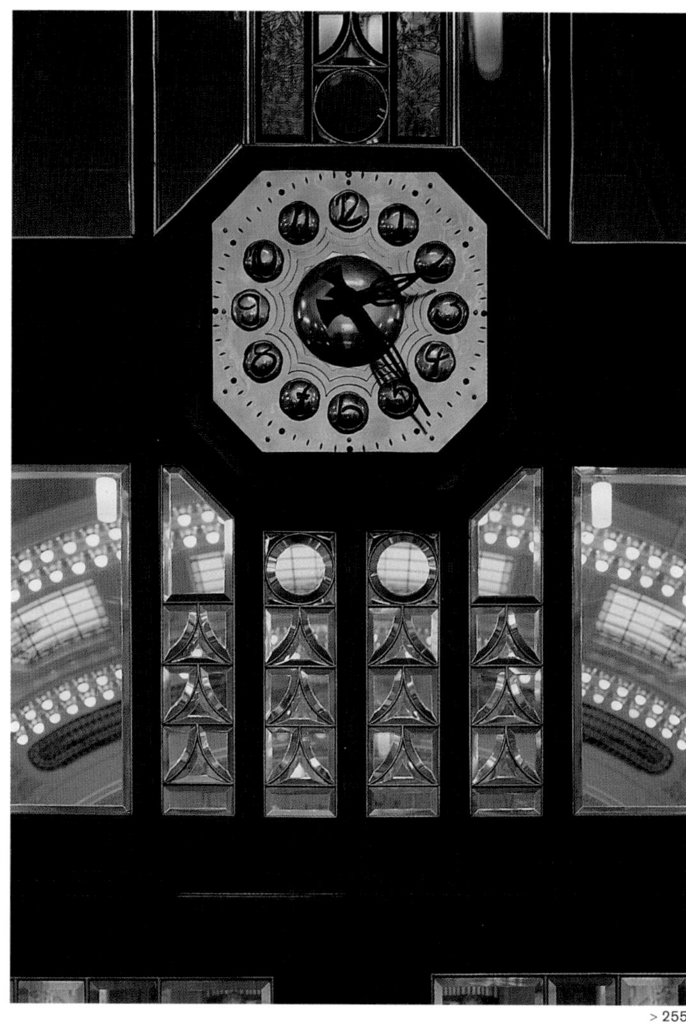

> 255

254 < Column capital and stucco decoration of the foyer
255 > Clock in the glass-panel entrance into Smetana Hall
256 > Detail of a door into Smetana Hall

> 256

> 257

> 258

257 < View of the foyer towards Smetana Hall
258 > View of the foyer facing the Mayor's Hall

> 259

> 260

259 < Lighting unit in the foyer
260 < Lighting unit in the corridor
261 > Lighting unit in the corridor outside Grégr Hall
262 > View of a lighting unit when looking from the corridor to the mezzanine
263 > Band of lights on the girder of the foyer ceiling

> 261

> 262

> 263

> 264

264 << View of the foyer from the corridor outside Sladkovský Hall
265 << View of the foyer from the stairway

266 > Detail of wrought grill
267 > Railing of a balcony on the mezzanine
268 > Detail of the figural decoration of the landing between the first and second floors
269 > Landing with a mirror and sculpted decoration by Antonín Štrunc

270 >> Side wall of the foyer of the first floor with the elevator door and entrance to the stairway
271 >> View of the second floor from the landing

> 266

> 267

> 268

> 270

Mayor's Hall

This circular hall has a privileged location above the main entrance. Situated in the center of the front façade, it is ingeniously separated from the balcony above the front marquee by a glass window wall, ornate with violet stained-glass windows that let mysterious cool light into the room. This is true not only when it is sunny but also when the weather is rather dull and even at night when the colored stained-glass windows filter the street light, just as their genius creator intended.
The intricate decoration of the hall is a complex work of the world-renowned Alfons Mucha. It is no exaggeration that the ceremonial luxury of the Mayor's Hall makes it the most impressive interior of the Municipal House. The hall's motif of Slavonic concord and its emphasis on the traditions and historical roots of the Czech nation is not only the focus of the interior of the Mayor's Hall, but national self-determination is also the main idea of the entire Municipal House, built in the center of multinational culture of the then Austro-Hungarian Empire and particularly German-oriented Prague.
When the structure was being designed and built, Alfons Mucha was already working on the cycle called "The Slavonic Epic". The ideas of the architects of the Municipal House were very familiar to him. He was living in Paris, getting ready to go to the U.S.A. on business at that time. After his return to his homeland in 1910, he began work and on January 25, 1911, the final designs for the hall were approved in his studio. While he was still alive, Mucha exhibited the designs for the Municipal House (which were the property of the city) both at home and abroad. Named "Sacrifice", "By Our Own Strength", and "Masculinity", three murals and a lot of preparatory studies and sketches were presented.
The ceremonial Mayor's Hall, as has been said, is situated in the main façade axis. It is of a circular plan, but its space "opens" toward the wall with windows. It is vaulted by a shallow dome, supported by eight pendetives with lunettes in the arcades between the pillars. The window recesses allowed two other, prominent lunettes.
Mucha's best work, from the artistic point of view, in which he came closest to his Art-Nouveau style, is the central ceiling fresco called "The Slavonic Concord". Figural motifs are arranged in a circle, the center of which is dominated by the wings of a flying eagle that seems to "shield" the solidarity. The fresco is framed by a silver-plated garland.
The three aforementioned murals illustrate the author's words: "Oh, Holy Mother of the Nation – accept the love and fervor of your son!", "With strength towards freedom – with love towards concord!" and "Humiliated and tortured – you shall be resurrected, my orphaned country!" The murals on the pendetives are linked to the ideas of civil virtues, which Mucha presents personified in famous Czech historical figures (Fidelity – J. A. Comenius, Creative Power – Jan of Pernštejn, Vigilance – the Chods, Resolution – Jan Roháč of Dubá, Independence – Jiří of Poděbrady, Justice – Master Jan Hus, Maternal Wisdom – Eliška Přemyslovna, Militancy – Jan Žižka).
The pilasters are decorated by Art-Nouveau mascarons of silver-plated stucco. The top part conceals lights that provide indirect illumination for the arches, while the lower part has silver-plated wall fixtures with layers of cascading glass lusters. The lower parts of the pilasters are wainscoted with artificial ochre marble and squares of different colors affixed to the wall. Mirrors situated on the radiator covers of marble, with brass decorative grills, enhance the effect of the wainscoting. The mirrors make the hall seem larger and give the room a feeling of mystery, intensifying the feeling of luxury and sacredness. Small side pillars carry busts and triangular pediments (bearing the name of the mural), completed with grills and sconces.
The balcony door and windows in the main façade, designed by Mucha, are decorated with stained-glass windows with motifs of snakes, doves, and botanical elements, carried out by the Staněk & Šebek company. The color hues are not arbitrary – blue represents the pre-historical times and purple-red stands for power and glory of the Middle Ages. The interior is completed by restored hangings with rich embroidery, fringes, and metal appliqués with tassels. As a novelty, aluminum, which had just been "discovered" at that time, was used, as its lightness enabled the artist to incorporate larger metal decorations into functioning textiles. These heavy hangings of felt-based material cover the side, semicircular doorways leading into Rieger Hall and Palacký Hall.

> 272

272 << View of Riegr Hall when looking from Palacký Hall through the Mayor's Hall

273 > Windows of the Mayor's Hall and door to main the balcony

274 > View of the windows with stained-glass decoration

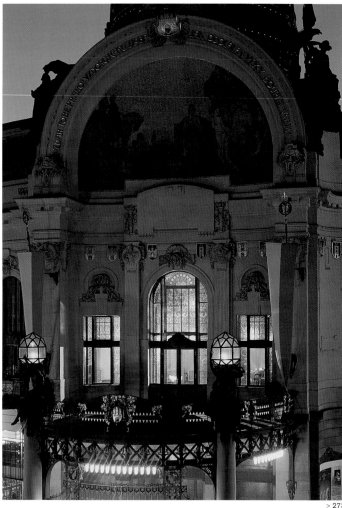

> 273

The peacock motifs are a remainder of Mucha's decorating of Fouquet's jewelry store in Paris. The hangings were made according to Mucha's design by the City Industrial Continuing School.

An inseparable part of the original interior of the hall is the furniture made of black-stained oak, gilded with silver leaf, and made by Josef Krejčík. The mat gilding technology was typically used on sumptuous catafalques – here, in the interior, it was used to enhance the ceremonial character of the whole hall. It raises the quality of "ordinary" wood to the cool delicacy of marble. Two seating units built in the window recesses are also very ornate. They create a whole with the radiator covers, into which Mucha's decorative panels "The Crown of Bohemia" and "Weeping over the Ruin of the Country" are incorporated. By their contradicting character the two motifs present the spirit of the Mayor's Hall decoration – patriotic optimism and pessimism. Interestingly shaped floor lamps are an inseparable part of the benches.

The seating of the main room is effected by movable armchairs of black and silver wood, upholstered with elegant green leather bordered with silver studs. The arrangement of the chairs, one of which has a strikingly taller back, was usually in a circle or ellipse, and the number depended on the type of the event. The arrangement could be completed with a table whose surface is rounded along the lengthwise edges.

The wings of the door are harmonized with the marble wainscoting of the walls that contain the same symbols as the other wooden interior elements. They are decorated with iron fittings and handles made of white metal (the other side of the door has differently wrought fittings as well as the colors of the metal and wood).

The floor is made of off-white marble with an attractive border in terra cotta and gray hues. We know from period photographs that for special occasions it would be covered with a Persian carpet, but this was obviously not a part of Mucha's original design.

When enumerating all the elements of the Mayor's Hall decoration, we have to keep in mind the intended complexity of the entire space, its strong ideological intention, and poetic subtext. All of the decorative elements are a part of a complex piece of art and tend towards the effect of harmonized morphology both in content and color scheme. The color symbolism – black, expressing the burden of subjugation, yellow, evoking the feeling of freedom and liberation – comes not only from the historical meaning of the color moods, but also expresses the author's patriotic state of mind and intensifies the dramatic atmosphere of his decorative plan. All of this is an outcome of the longing for national identity at the time of the construction of the Municipal House based on Slavonic accord and our own history.

> 274

BO
JOV
NOST
SYNA SVÉHO
SVATÁ MATKO NÁRODA
PŘIJMI LÁSKU A NADŠENÍ!

275 << View of the door to Palacký Hall

276 > View from the entrance from the first-floor foyer
277 > Walls with a mirror and entrances to Palacký Hall and the first-floor foyer

> 276

> 277

278 > Detail of the mirror frame decoration
279 > Allegory of civic virtues, Creative Power – Jan of Pernštejn

> 278

280–282 > Details of the decoration with mascarons and indirect lighting of the inscriptions
283 > Ceiling decoration by Alfons Mucha, in the center the allegory of the Slavonic Concord, on the pendetives civic virtues

> 280

> 281

> 282

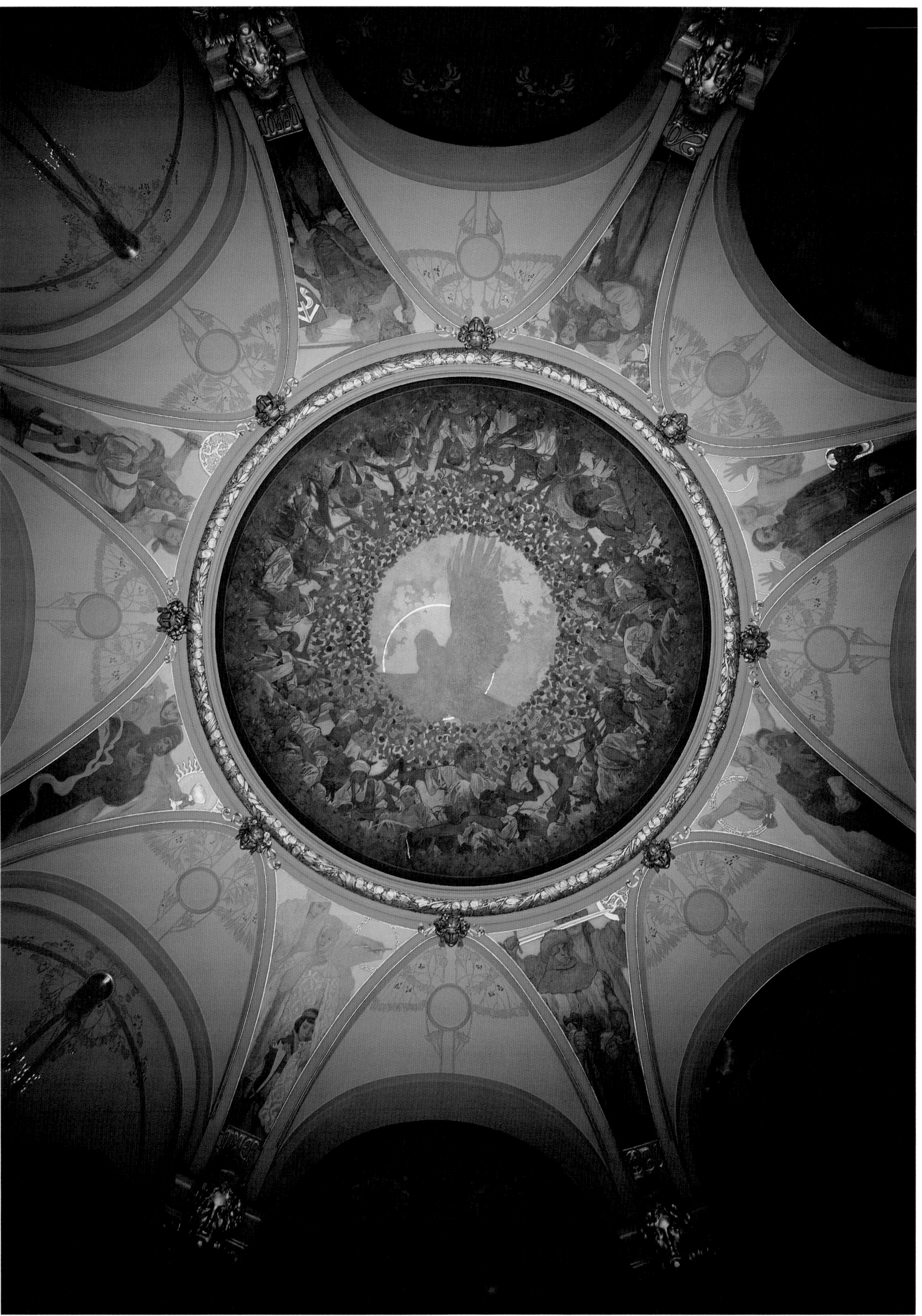

> 284

284 < Alfons Mucha, With strength towards freedom – with love towards concord!, detail of a lunette
285 > Alfons Mucha, Maternal Wisdom – Eliška Přemyslovna, detail (prince Václav, later, the emperor Charles IV)
286 > Alfons Mucha, Independence – Jiří of Poděbrady, detail

> 285

> 286

287 > Alfons Mucha, Independence – Jiří of Poděbrady, detail
288 > Alfons Mucha, Justice – Master Jan Hus, detail
289 > Alfons Mucha, Maternal Wisdom – Eliška Přemyslovna, detail

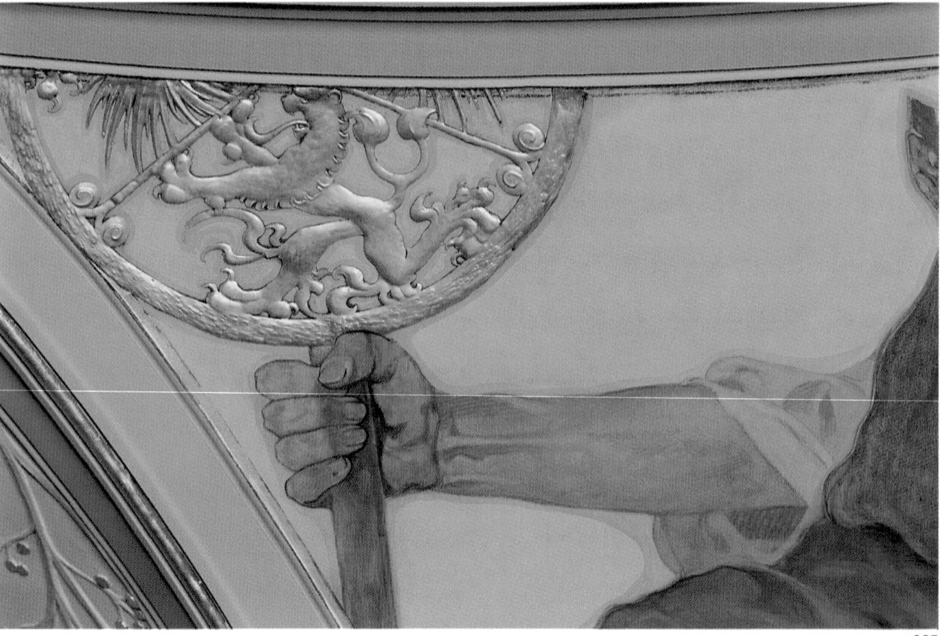

> 287

> 288

> 289

> 290

290 < Ceiling decoration with Alfons Mucha's allegory of Justice – Master Jan Hus

291 > Alfons Mucha, Militancy – Jan Žižka, detail

292 > Alfons Mucha, Resolution – Jan Roháč of Dubá

> 291

> 292

293 < Seating unit in the window niche with a picture of the Czech Crown by Alfons Mucha

> 294

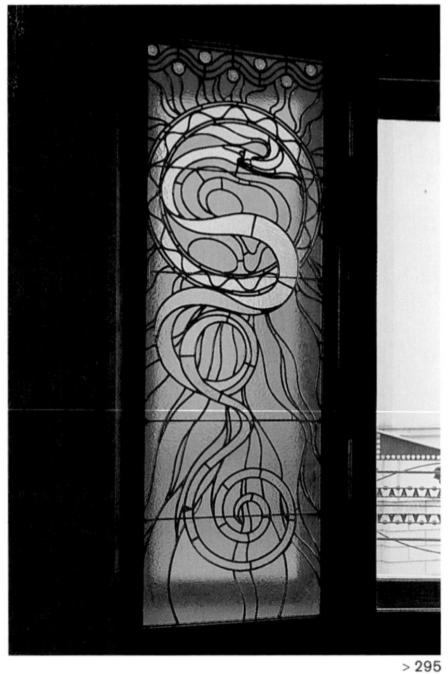

> 295

> 296

294–296 < Details of the stained-glass windows
297 > Detail of a sofa and a niche by the window

SYNA SVÉHO
SVATÁ MATKO NÁRODA
PŘIJMI LÁSKU A NADŠENÍ
VĚR
NOST

> 298

NEPOD

> 300

298 << Wall with a mirror and a painting by Alfons Mucha called Oh, Holy Mother of the Nation – accept the love and fervor of your son!

299 << Window niche with a seating unit and a painting by Alfons Mucha called Weeping over the ruin of the country

300 < Entrance to Riegr Hall with a hanging

301 > Detail of the hanging

> 301

> 302

> 303

> 304

302–307 < Details of the door hangings

> 305

> 306

> 307

SILOU
K SVOBODĚ - LÁSKOU K

308 < View of the main entrance with the triptych of murals in the lunettes and with allegories of the civic virtues by Alfons Mucha

Palacký Hall

Next to the mystic atmosphere of the Mayor's Hall lies a freshly illuminated hall with two window axes. The hall is square with a simple trough vault with lunettes.

The central octagonal area of the ceiling is adorned with a painting by Jan Preisler called "A Girl and Flying Birds", which is bordered with gilded sculpted decoration, placed in the square frame of the ceiling. The space is embellished with relief molding and small sunken squares with hanging bulbs. It is important to remember here the period's enchantment with the electric light bulb. Compared to the usual gas light, the bright electric light was at the beginning of the 20th century quite miraculous. The creators and the author of the painted decoration apparently intended to achieve the most intense direct light possible in order to brighten the room and fill it with light. For this purpose, clear bulbs are the ideal, literally sparkling, source of light.

To enhance this feeling, subtle-looking brass chandeliers with glass chains and cut, cascading lusters were mounted in the corner coffers of the ceiling. The lunettes and the outside perimeter of the ceiling bay are bordered with gilded bands of stylized rocaille ornaments. The vaulting cells are decorated with coiling acanthus leaves, painted around an ornate, circular brass grill.

The walls are smooth with artificial marble wainscoting of a light ochre hue and completed with a bottom segment in a dark crimson and a plinth in a dark green. The wall that neighbors Grégr Hall has three glass-paneled doors with brass handles of extraordinary quality. The walls with the opposing entrances have semicircular fanlights decorated with geometrical clear glass and set in brass frames.

In the window wall axis, placed on a marble pedestal, there is a bronze bust of František Palacký (1798–1876), an important Czech historian, politician, philosopher, and organizer of national culture, who was called "the father of the country" for his achievements. The bust was made by Josef Václav Myslbek in 1885.

Two murals on the wall opposite the windows, painted by Jan Preisler in 1910–1912, dominate the hall. The murals depict figural scenes in dreamlike countrysides. The first mural with the motif of bathing women is filled with heavenly calm and static quiet. The second one depicts a victorious young man with a lance, riding a white horse and surrounded by groups of men and women. The pastel sketches and studies for the figures are housed in the Gallery of the City of Prague. In creating his harmonious composition, Jan Preisler, influenced by the broad-mindedness of the pictures by Puvis de Chavannes and Nicolas Poussin, was attempting to solve new formal problems of art, in which young Czech artists were also interested. Next to the entrance to the Mayor's Hall, two original, uniquely large, beveled, frameless mirrors are fitted. Their perfection and size creates authentic reflections of the murals, so the visitor at first believes that there is another wall with murals. The wooden frames of the upholstered sofas by Josef Krejčík, placed under these mirrors, are adorned with gilded carved figures. The gilding was restored according to period photographs.

> 310

> 311

310 < View of Jan Preisler's painting and a mirror
(reflecting the painting)
311 > Detail of the ceiling decoration with a row of lights

312–314 > Stucco decoration of the ceiling, details
315 > The Hall's ceiling with a painting by Jan Preisler

> 312

> 313

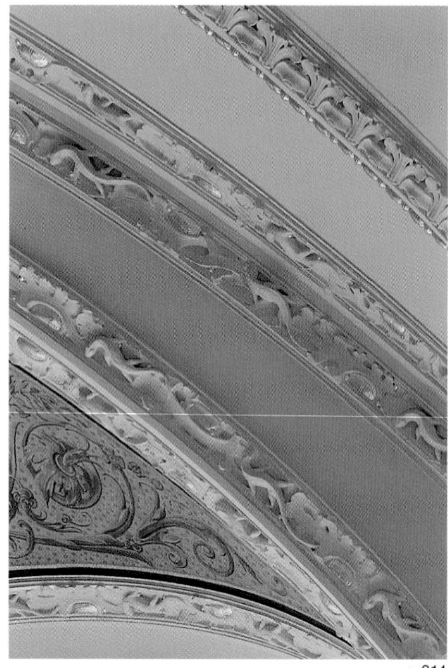
> 314

> 316

> 317

316 < Door handle from the door to Grégr Hall, detail
317 > Reliefs on the sofa
318 > Sofa
319 > Sofa leg

> 318

> 319

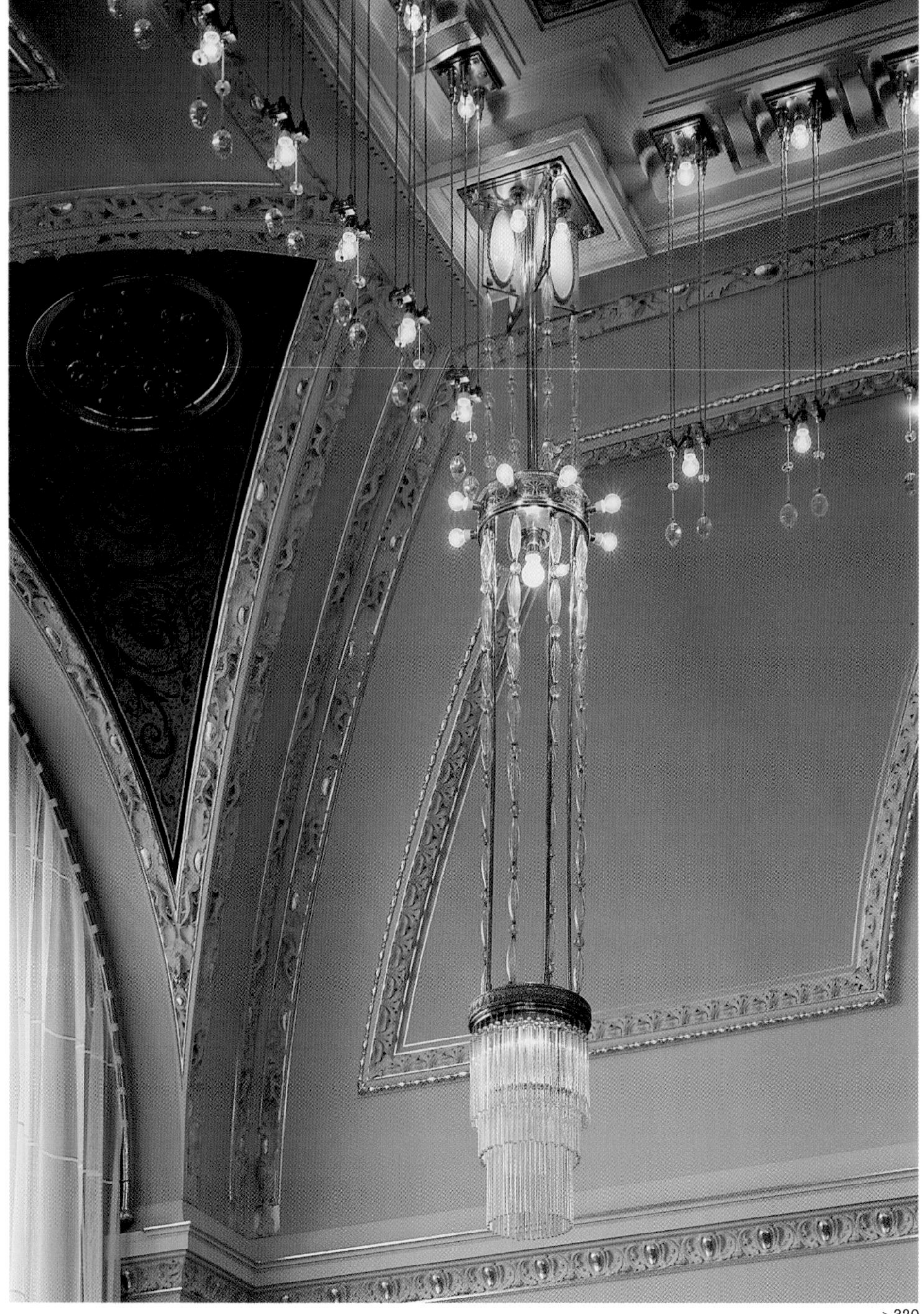

> 320

320 > The Hall's lighting

321 > View of the door to Grégr Hall

SÁL PALACKÉHO

Grégr Hall

This spacious rectangular hall was named after a prominent Czech politician of the 19th century, co-founder of the National Liberal Party ("Young Czechs"), and founder of the National Newspaper, Doctor Julius Grégr. His bust by Emanuel Halman is situated on a bracket between the windows. Originally, it was designed as a meeting and party hall, and so there is a raised stage and gallery for musicians.

The first impression will take us back to the 19th century – several decades before the high Art-Nouveau style and the construction of the Municipal House. The general color scheme, structure, and materials used, with the dominating geometrical ornaments of the artificial marble wainscoting and large murals, will make us imagine the period of the construction of the city theaters and pompous palaces for cultural purposes, as they were built around almost all Europe. The leading author of the decoration, František Ženíšek, is usually placed in the so-called "Generation of the National Theater", in the second half of the 19th century.

It is quite interesting to note that several generations of artists were given a chance to participate in the decoration of the Municipal House. This unique, non-conflicting cooperation of such diverse artists was enabled only thanks to the idea of the construction of this building: a presentation of the national visual art and architecture to support the patriotic identity.

The result is an ideological variety of artistic concepts and architectural articulation, which is, particularly in this hall, multiplied since we enter from the neighboring airy and freshly decorated Palacký Hall.

The variety in the design of these two neighboring halls is not diminished even by their identical large windows in subtle oak frames, which after almost 100 years needed only slight restoration and were preserved in functional condition, including the brass fittings.

The spacious flat ceiling is designed in a typical way as a three-part composition with beams with framed edges that form brackets when they meet the walls. Rectangular brass ventilation grills are placed between them. The ceiling segments are decorated simply with geometric relief, gilded rectangles, rhomboids, and oval lenses. The whole ceiling articulation is highly decorative due to the fact that the ceiling framework is made of the modern steel structure just like the rest of the building. It is useful to remember, being in this somewhat historicizing hall, that from the architectural point of view the Municipal House is a modern building, during whose construction the most recent architectural knowledge and technical equipment was used. The building is only "dressed" in an earlier or period "coat". The chosen concept was able to prove the capability of Czech authors – artists and craftsmen – and comprehensively demonstrate everything as comparable to other European cultures and, at the same time, present the Czech national identity.

The ceiling paintings by František Ženíšek symbolizing "Life", "Poetry", and "Death" are bordered with a band of geometrical elements. The stucco decoration of the ceiling was carried out by Antonín Novák. The large rectangular lighting units, hung on brass rods, make an original element of the hall's decoration. They consist of wrought brass-sheet blocks with glass panes and glass lenses. The chandeliers with long lusters of beads and wands were made by František Křižík.

The major work of art in the hall is a mural triptych, which was painted on canvas and glued to the wall. It has a stucco frame with marble decoration and gilding. The paintings cover the whole area of the long wall opposite the windows. They depict the stages of life from birth to death. The symbolic names "Love Song", "War Song", and "Funeral Song" capture the interest of the author of the Municipal House decoration – he offered to paint six allegorical paintings and asked Mikoláš Aleš to cooperate on them. Aleš, however, refused. František Ženíšek turned in the sketches for the mural triptych to the supervisory board for the Municipal House construction prior to October 15, 1910. The final sketches were approved on December 23, 1911. The actual execution of the paintings dragged as well, and so the mural triptych was completed after the opening of the Municipal House. The third painting, "Funeral Song", was completed by the artist's pupils.

The walls between the paintings and on the window pillars are wainscoted in artificial marble in basic ochre hues. The wainscoting consists of vertical panels in most of the hall and covers a large part of the north wall. The wainscoting under the paintings is carried out in illusory geometrical shapes in terra cotta, dark green, and gray colors. The pilasters

322 > View of the door to Palacký Hall
323 > View of the platform

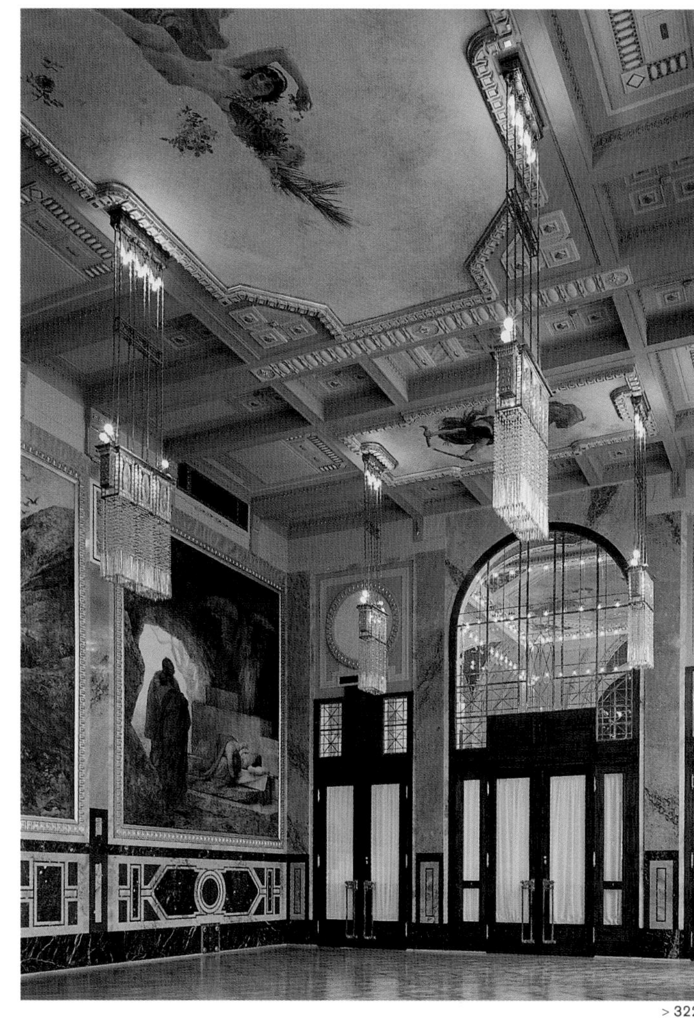

> 322

projecting from the walls are topped with illusory capitals. The front wall of the hall, above the wooden stage, is wainscoted with artificial marble of similar colors. It is articulated into frames bordering three openings. The left one is blind, the middle one has a relief panel door, and the right entrance has mirrors in a small, grill-like articulation. Through the middle door, one can enter a clubroom designed in the place of the altered corridor to the Powder Tower. In the present day it functions as a waiting room for participating performers.

A large, segmented balcony arches above the stage. It has brass light fittings with lusters and an ornamental brass railing, made by Alois Čada, and is embellished with textile hangings with appliqués and fringes, which correspond to the textile window drapes. They are, together with the lace curtains, modern replicas of original features, added later according to period photographs.

> 323

SAL PALACKEHO

324 < View of the Mayor's Hall from Grégr Hall through Palacký Hall

> 324

> 325

325 < Detail of the wall with glass panes above the middle door into Palacký Hall
326 > Main chandeliers, detail
327 > Lighting unit above the platform
328 > Lighting unit above the balcony

> 326

> 327

> 328

> 329

> 330

> 331

329 < Wainscoting on the pillar between windows, detail
330 < Wainscoting of the hall, detail
331 < Door from the platform to the corridor to the Powder Tower
332 > František Ženíšek, Life, painting on ceiling
333 > František Ženíšek, Death, painting on ceiling
334 > Stucco decoration of the ceiling

> 332

> 333

> 334

> 336

335 << Diagonal view of František Ženíšek's painting Love Song, and a part of the painting War Song

336 < View of the platform with a balcony
337 > Open gallery of the corridor to the Powder Tower
338 > Clubroom in the corridor to the Powder Tower (one of the walls is formed by the Tower's elevation)

> 337

> 338

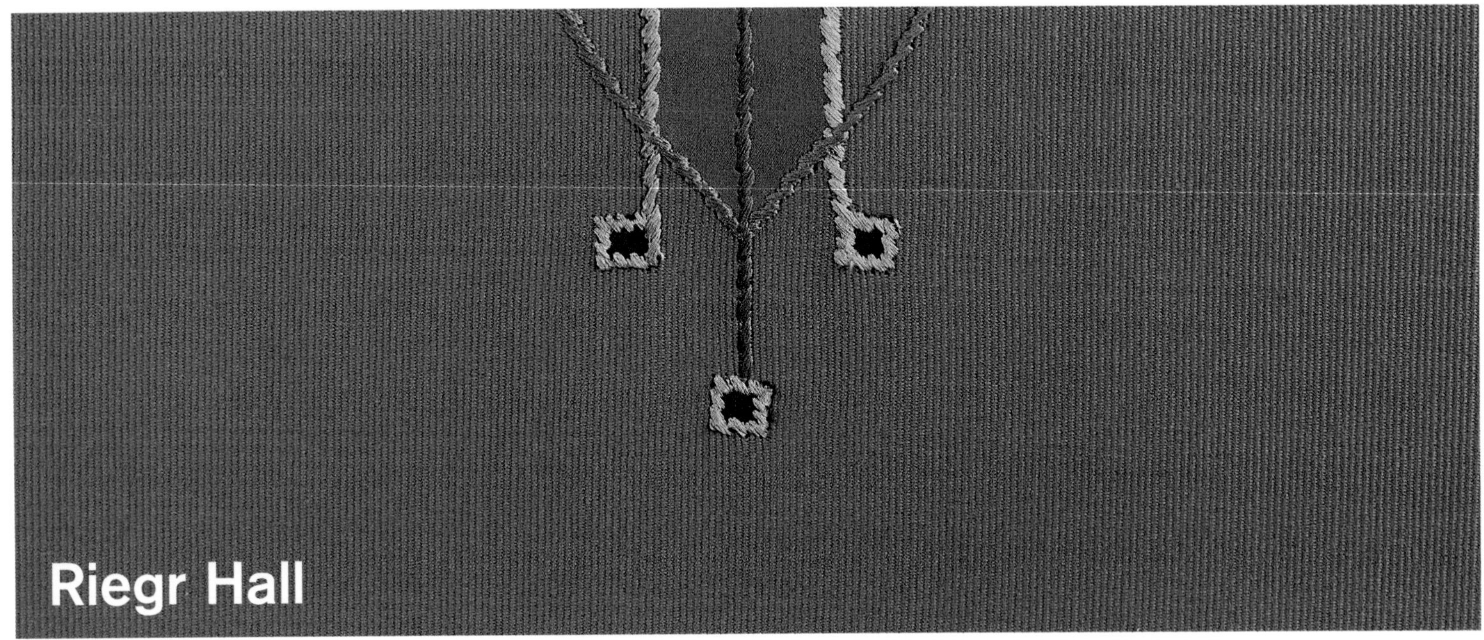

Riegr Hall

This ceremonial hall with patriotic decorations and luxurious furnishing competes with the Mayor's Hall in its revivalist character and lavishness. However, it does not evoke a sense of mystery in its depiction of Slavonic history, nor is it based on the same mysticism, evoking reality and longing for freedom. On the contrary, the hall is designed to present the most prominent figures of the Czech National Revival in a modern way. The floor plan of the hall is square, incorporating two windows of the main façade. These large windows provide a lot of light. The luxury and grandeur of the room is achieved by the implementation of splendid interior elements made of quality materials and by perfect workmanship.

The hall has a trough vault with lunettes and a square centerpiece, broken by two crossed beams into four coffers. The edges of the lunettes, which extend to the top of the walls' wainscoting, are bordered with moldings of stylized Art-Nouveau leaves and gilded fruit. The lunettes over the entryways are flanked by flat, decorative fillets, which are topped with sculpted wreaths around cameo-like medallions. The perimeter of the ceiling is bordered with a wide band of leafed twigs. The stucco decoration was done by Antonín Štrunc, according to Antonín Balšánek's design. Palace-type lighting units with pendants hang from the center of the cross and along the perimeter of the ceiling.

The main artistic decorations are two murals by Max Švabinský called "Czech Spring". The murals are a synthesis of portraits of the prominent figures of Czech literature (Svatopluk Čech, Jan Neruda, Jaroslav Vrchlický, Božena Němcová, Julius Zeyer), the visual arts (sculptor Josef Václav Myslbek and painters Mikoláš Aleš and Josef Mánes), and world-famous musical composers Bedřich Smetana and Antonín Dvořák. From extant documents we know that the creation of this monumental decorative piece, in which the artist had to combine with plausibility and realism the different portraits as though in a moment of casual meeting, was of the greatest importance to him. Some of the portrait sketches, which were created prior to the painting, reside in the collections of the National Gallery.

Placed between the two murals is the bust of a leading politician and representative of the National Party ("Old Czechs"), Doctor František Ladislav Riegr (1818–1903), made by Josef Václav Myslbek. The pedestal is of crimson marble and sits in a niche lined with ceramic mosaic. A marble plaque with an excerpt from Riegr's argument at the gathering of the Assembly of the Czech Kingdom (February 25, 1867) is set into the wall paneling. Under the orders of the Protectorate officials the plaque was covered in 1940, and it consequently was not discovered until 1990.

The dark oak wainscoting, carved and inlaid with small motifs, and the furnishings built into the walls (the bookcase, sofa, and pedestals next to the entrance to Sladkovský Hall) were made by Jan Navrátil. The bookcase has a tomb-shaped base, adorned with ornamental ironwork, three cases, fronted with glass-filled brass frames, and a stepped pyramid along the top, on which is set a wooden sculpture by Josef Pekárek, entitled "Prague". In contrast with the adjoining Mayor's Hall, where the wood is done in black and silver, the oak, stained with warm colors and gold powder, is both shiny and ceremonial. The panels in the wooden wainscoting and the seating units have been recently re-upholstered with replicas of the original ornaments, embroidery, and fringes. A mirror, set in a carved and inlaid wooden frame with a gilded war slogan, "We shall persevere", faces Riegr's bust, and is on the central pillar between the windows.

The areas around the entryways are also quite ornate. The lower parts are decorated with small glass panes in brass frames and with carved garlands, and the arch of glass over the door is broken by a series of vertical bands. On the north side, there is a garland with stained glass.

SÁL
:RIEGRŮV:

> 340

Text on the marble plaque:

"THE SOVEREIGN RIGHT OF THE CZECH CROWN HAS A FIRM BASIS, IT IS AN UNDENIABLE DEED, IT IS THE RESULT OF MANY YEARS, EVEN THOUSANDS OF YEARS OF OUR NATION'S ACTIVITY. IT IS THE RESULT OF GREAT BATTLES, OFTEN HEROIC AND VICTORIOUS, OFTEN UNFORTUNATE, BUT ALWAYS HONEST, WHICH OUR NATION UNDERTOOK TO DEFEND ITS INDIVIDUALITY AND ITS POLITICAL IDENTITY. THIS POLITICAL IDENTITY, THIS INDIVIDUALITY, WE HAVE PRESERVED UNTIL THESE DAYS, AND WE WOULD BETRAY OUR FOREFATHERS IF WE WANTED TO ABANDON IT OF OUR OWN FREE WILL AND SET OFF INTO SOMETHING QUITE UNCERTAIN AND UNSTABLE. THESE THINGS, NAMELY THE SOVEREIGN RIGHT AND THE POLITICAL IDENTITY OF THE CZECH KINGDOM, ARE PRICELESS, EVEN DEAR TO US ABOVE ALL."

> 341

339 << View of the entrance from the Mayor's Hall

340 < View of the wall with lunette paintings by Max Švabinský called the Czech Spring

341 > František Ladislav Riegr's bust by Josef Václav Myslbek

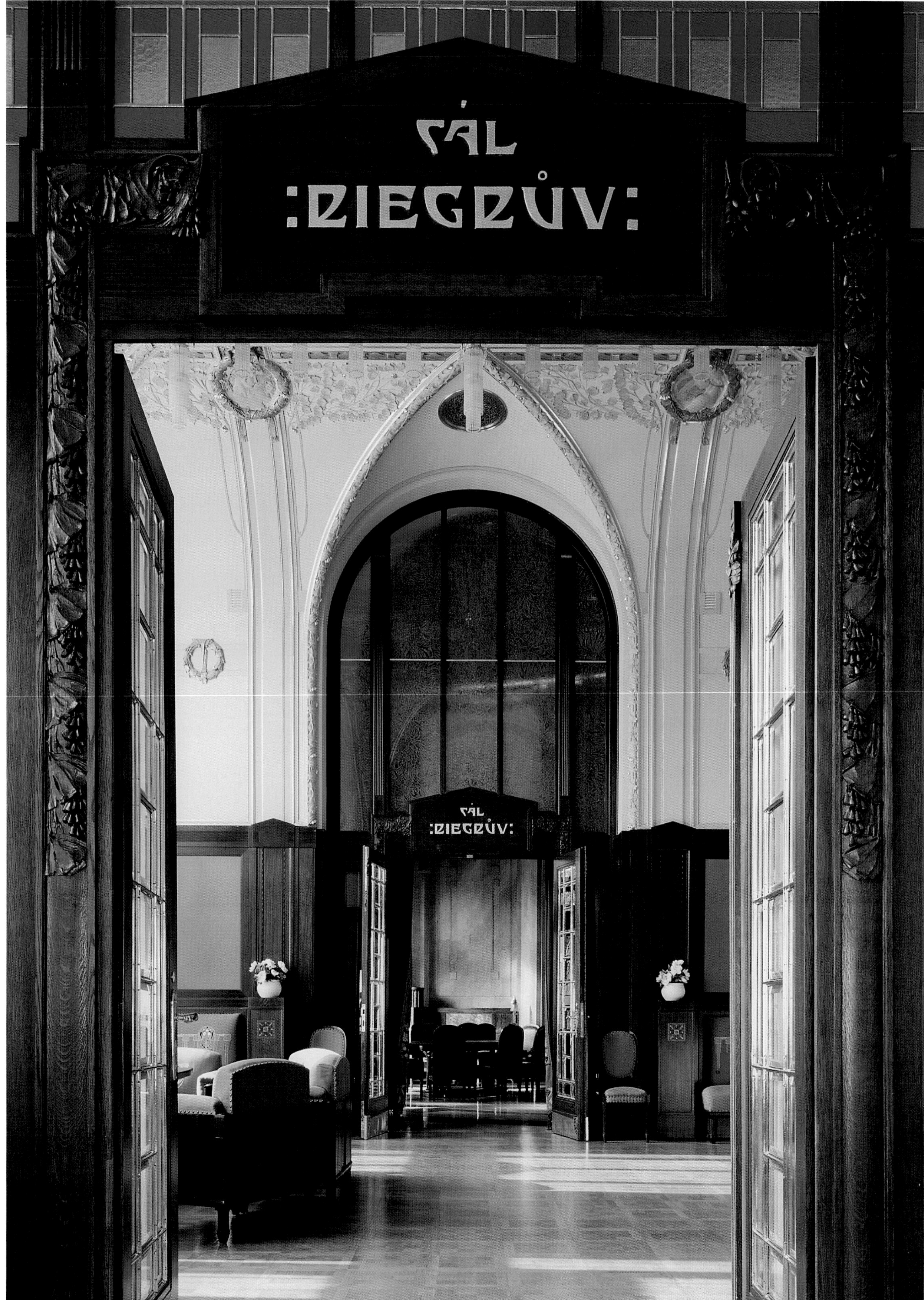

> 342

342 < View of the Mayor's Hall from Sladkovský Hall through Riegr Hall
343 > Upholstered furniture with ornamental appliqués and embroidery

> 344

344 < Seating unit by the window
345 > Sofas by the wall with the bust of F. L. Riegr
346 > Bookcase with a sculpture by Josef Pekárek called Prague

347 >> Detail of the hall's ceiling with lighting units
348 >> Table and a part of the seating unit

> 345

> 346

> 347

> 348

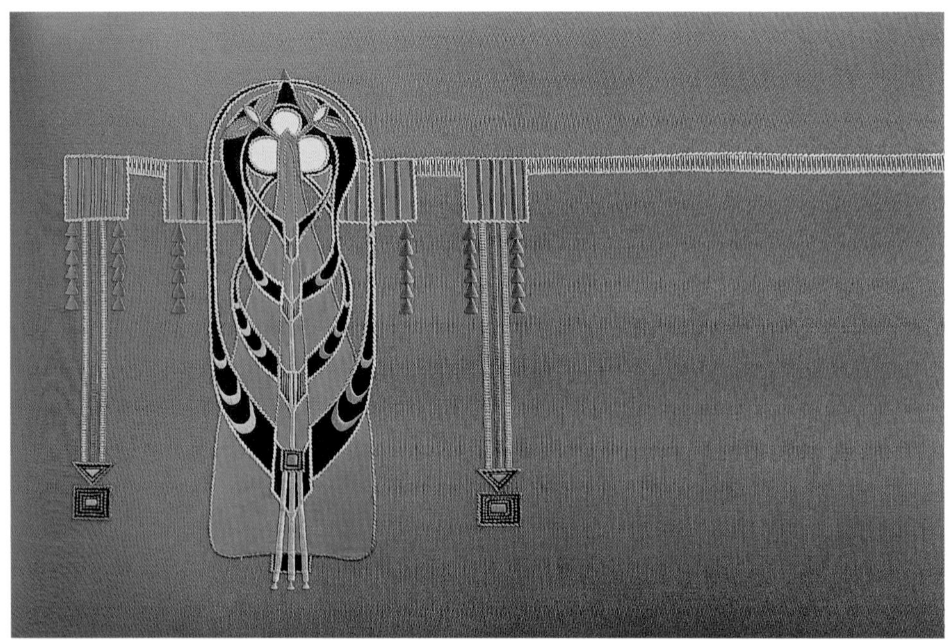

> 349

> 350

349–350 < Appliqués and embroidery of the upholstery, details
351 > Ceramic tiling of a niche behind the bust
352–353 > Inlaid wooden wainscoting, details

> 351

> 352

> 353

NEDEJME SE

354 < Original seating unit in front of a mirror with Riegr's motto: "We shall persevere"

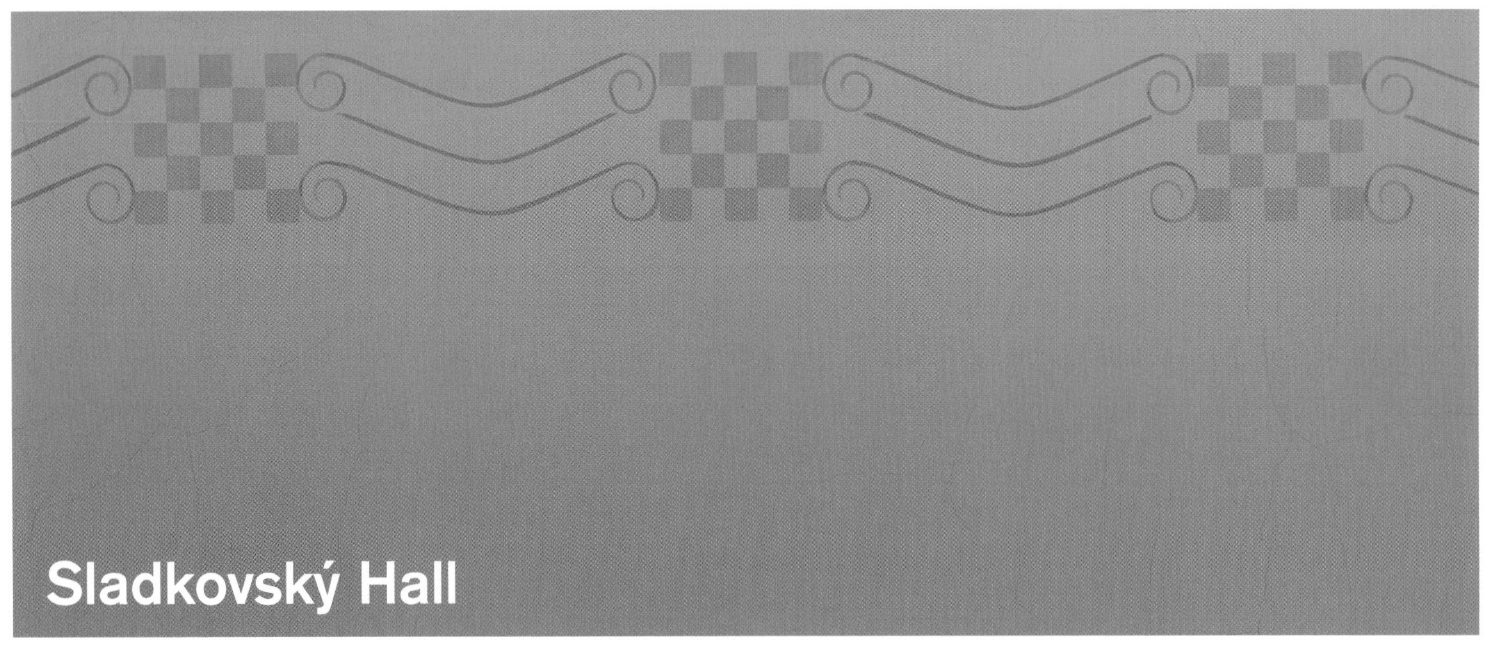

Sladkovský Hall

The hall was originally designed as a lecture hall, or in today's terminology, a conference hall. It is rectangular in shape and rather long. A small parlor at the north end of the room adds further to its length. The parlor itself is one-half meter higher than the rest of the hall, and can thus serve as a platform or a stage.

Compared to the other halls of the first floor, the room is designed in a simple, modest fashion, without embellishing paintings or picture decorations. Originally, it was intended to be adorned with a cycle of murals, but they were never painted, so the walls were stenciled instead. In such an austere setting, the well-designed proportions of the room stand out, particularly the harmonized row of large windows, the high-reaching wainscoting on the opposite wall, partitioned by several doorways, the stained glass over the entryway, and the major chandeliers augmented by ranks of ceiling lighting units. Even this modest hall is imbued with a ceremonial atmosphere, which is particularly impressive during conferences, ball, or dance lessons, since the furniture can either be fitted to the purpose of the event or completely removed. The simplicity of the room sets off the luxurious details of the period craftsmanship, i.e., the embroidered curtains, the decorative clock, various brass air vents, the quality parquet floor, and original bentwood chairs.

The hall has a flat ceiling, divided by raised crossbeams. Fluted stucco bands run the length of the room and are crossed by paneled beams that continue as lesenes down the walls. Under the ceiling, they are decorated with stylized motifs of linden twigs with polychrome coats-of-arms of the city of Prague.

The front wall that separates the raised "parlor" from the rest of the room is divided into three parts. The central section consists of a dominating arch, springing from the carved wooden wainscoting, whose archivolt is comprised of moldings with botanical elements. At the top of the arch, in the voussoir, there is an Art-Nouveau mascaron crowned with linden leaves. The side entrances to the platform are rectangular in shape. The rectangular segments of the wall above them have stucco decoration and striking round brass rosette-shaped grills.

The original decorative brass chandeliers are fitted in the intersections of the ceiling beams. From their square base, a faceted lantern is lowered, which in turn supports a large wrought ring with lights and glass lusters. The wainscoting of natural oak reaches to the height of the doorways. It is articulated by sunken rectangles, raised disks, and carved cable molding. Above the doors, the wainscoting is connected with a shaped band. The doors have beveled glass panes set in brass frames. Mirrors are attached to the pillars of the window wall and in the wooden wainscoting between the doors. Brass three-part lighting units on cantilevers with lusters are fitted above the mirrors.

The hall is furnished mainly with chairs. The original chairs are impressive not only for their aesthetic qualities but also for their craftsmanship. They have proved their high quality and durability through daily use in different halls of the building over the span of almost an entire century.

A bust made by Ladislav Kofránek of Doctor Karel Sladkovský (1823–1880), a brilliant speaker, important politician and a member of the radical Czech movement of 1848, is placed on the hall platform, or in the raised parlor, which was called the "Committee Room" in the original plans.

The ceiling is adorned with a molded, rectangular, segmented frame and gilded Art-Nouveau botanical stucco decoration. The lighting units with glass lusters are fitted in two rows along the main axis and in the corners of the ceiling. The parlor receives its character mainly from the restored original wallpaper with Art-Nouveau décor, which is supposed to imitate silk. Colored, geometrical stained-glass panels are inserted in the wooden wainscoting. The major element of the room is a tomb-shaped radiator cover with a mirror tabernacle. Above the mirror is a landscape painting by Josef Ullmann. The cover has a richly decorative brass grill, made by Alois Čada, and a marble mantelpiece. The overall impression is completed with blue textile drapes with appliqués and fringes, hanging in front of the windows and in the front arch, where they separate the main hall from the parlor. A brass decorative clock hangs from the arch as well. The curtains were designed specifically to fit the decoration pattern of the hall.

> 356

> 357

355 <<< View of the platform with the "Committee Room"

356 << View into the hall from the platform

357 < View of the entrance to Riegr Hall
358 > Vent grill on the platform
359 > Wainscoting on the pillar by the platform, with a relief
360 > Stained-glass pane of the door to the dining parlors

> 358

> 359

> 360

361 > Clock in the platform doorway
362 > Lighting unit above a mirror
363 > Air vent grill above the side entrance to the platform
364 > Platform (originally "Committee Room"), detail of a ceiling with a chandelier

> 361

> 362

> 363

> 364

> 365

365 < Stucco decoration of the platform doorway, detail
366 > Stained glass of the door to Riegr Hall, detail
367 > Decoration of the drapes in the platform doorway, detail
368 > Curtains in the hall, detail

> 366

> 367

> 368

369 > Radiator cover on the platform with a landscape painting by Josef Ullmann
370 > Wooden wainscoting with a mirror
371 > View of the wooden wainscoting

> 369

> 370

SÁL
:RIEGRŮV:

> 372

372 < View of the hall with original chairs

Smetana Hall

Smetana Concert Hall fills out the central interior of the Municipal House in an intriguing way, stretching up from the first floor to the roof space, with the balcony extending over the entrance foyer. Due to its spaciousness and the round vaulting of the ceiling, as well as the refined lighting by lines of cut-glass lights, combined with the daylight penetrating through the ceiling, the hall gives today's visitor the impression of a large spaceship. Smetana Hall is indisputably valuable, not only thanks to the decoration and acoustics, but also because of its construction, daring for its time, which boldly made use of the possibilities of the then-modern riveted steel to vault the huge space. The overall impression of this hall, even after ninety years, is that of a pleasant, modern interior that complements the gracefulness of classical music, invoked by the presence of a large organ in the front of the hall. The organ serves a double function, as it also imparts to the viewer the timeless impression of a mystical temple.

The central part of the hall consists of a sail vault with a circular skylight dome on pendetives supported by massive pillars. The dome is filled with stained-glass panels and is flanked around the circumference by a band of richly ornate grills and a ring of lights. The ceiling is articulated by basket-arch portals with bands of lights. The lights are covered with clear-glass globes that reflect the rays into the hall around them as if they were pearl necklaces adorning the necks of elegant ladies. Colorful stained-glass windows and richly decorative grills, made by Alois Čada and Rudolf Šimůnek, are embedded in the vault bays between the portals. New lights, recreated according to photographs from the period, descend from the portal segments between the stained-glass windows. The lights, which are encased in spheres of milky-white glass and set in brass net, hang from wires decorated with portrayals of lyres.

The stage consists of two parts, the proscenium, which is raised 80 centimeters above the hall floor, and a semicircular organ loft with wooden choir gallery and railing, interesting because of its proportions. The organ pipes, supplied by Jan Tuček, are joined with a band, embellished with gilded medallions, bearing musical emblems. The central medallion, larger than the rest, is a depiction of Bedřich Smetana done by František Hergesel. An ochre textile curtain hangs from the portal in front of the organ. The front part of the stage, the orchestra area, is defined by high oak wainscoting that borders the proscenium. It consists of panels with sunken rectangles, populated with round lights, and flanked with carved bands. The woodwork was done by Jan Navrátil. Three-part galleries for the choir are situated on the side walls above the wainscoting, at the level of the first balcony. They are screened by louvers and embellished with a balustrade on the parapet and a sopraporta with putti and garlands under the highest gallery.

At the front of the hall is a portal bordered with gilded scale decoration, which separates the stage from the auditorium. The basket arch springers are embellished with cartouches with the coats-of-arms of Prague, adorned with an Art-Nouveau representation of leaves. The portal voussoir is accentuated by a composition of a cartouche and sitting female figure with two putti. Along the sides of the proscenium there are two large allegorical stucco sculptures by Ladislav Šaloun, called "Slavonic Dances" and "Vyšehrad". Between the stage portal and the main hall pillar, there is a section with a basket vault with colored stained-glass windows and three openings in the vertical wall.

The main floor of Smetana Hall can be entered from the first-floor hallways through glass doors, which have ornamental brass grill in the fanlights above. Both boxes – the president's and the mayor's – at the level of the first balcony are accentuated by the segmented arches of the balcony parapets and by an arcade archivolt above them, extended into a canopy with stucco decoration. The box draperies, with fringes, metal plaques, and tassels, are of ochre color. They are completed with lambrequins with appliqués of the city of Prague, embellished with embroidery and fringes, hanging down from the parapet. The second-level boxes are inserted in the arcade opening, reaching to the ceiling vault through lunettes. Inside, the arcade is decorated with drapery with appliqués and fringes.

The exedras of both side walls are defined by massive circular pillars, embedded in the walls. On the cornice, at the springing line of the vault, are decorative male and female sculptures by Karel Novák, who

373 << View of the rear of the hall with a pillar supporting the vault

> 374

collaborated with Ladislav Kofránek and Josef Kalvoda on the stucco decoration of the hall. Vertically the pillars hold three ranks of boxes. The pediment of the ground floor box is decorated with a wood paneled band with vent grills, which stretches along the stage front as well. The convex-shaped side balconies of the first-tier boxes are supported by small pillars from the ground floor, and so extend over the ground-floor boxes. At the tops of the pillars, draped putti "carry" the first-tier boxes. Along the bottom part of the side boxes, there is a decorative band of grills, sunken rectangular panels, and lights with lusters on cantilevers.
The ornate fronts of the box parapets and the parapet of the main balcony are embellished with the work of Josef Kalvoda, consisting of medallions of Czech music composers: Jan of Holešov, Bohuslav of Čechtice, Kryštof Harant of Polžice and Bezdružice, Václav Jan Tomášek, František Škroup, Vilém Blodek, Karel Bendl, and Zdeněk Fibich.
The balcony of the second-tier boxes arches above the side boxes of the first tier. It is carried by two female figures with undulating drapes and garlands, connected in the balcony center with a stucco lyre.
Along the sides of the boxes, Smetana Hall is decorated with murals by Karel Špillar – "Music", "Dance", "Poetry", and "Drama" – which belong among the author's best works. The tops of the exedras are decorated with gilded grills, and bands of lights border the arch edges. The lunettes, flanked with stucco molding, are filled with murals by Karel Špillar. The walls of the boxes and balcony are covered with a textured wallpaper of a miniature pattern in gold and decorated with large, beveled mirrors in wooden frames. The Thonet chairs are original, having been recently restored and newly upholstered.
The basket-arch portal of the niche above the main balcony is supported by two pillars with lights on cantilevers.
The ground-floor auditorium can be adjusted to the particular event by adding or removing sets of four folding seats which are not, unlike in single-purpose concert halls, firmly attached to the floor. They are designed so that they would be stable and comfortable, while enabling different orientations, to accommodate concert audiences, or, differently arranged, the spectators at fashion shows and other events. In addition, the hall can be supplied with conference or restaurant furniture, for balls, annual meetings, and other social events. The variability of furnishing and the high quality level floor make it possible to use this hall for almost any purpose.
In the back wall under the balcony, the exit into the main foyer with the exhibition halls is through four large oak doors. The perfectly crafted decorative brass fittings and beveled glass panels give the doors a luxurious feeling. The hall's main floor can be accessed through four additional doors along the perimeter. The boxes and balconies have their own entrances on different floors. As this is the most ceremonial of the Municipal House halls, one curiosity should be mentioned – the president's box is located on the left side of the stage in contradiction to world social conventions. It comes from a tradition from the time before the independent republic was established. According to this tradition, the most honorable place, that is the right side, was designated for the Mayor of Prague. At that time, Prague was only a provincial city of the Austro-Hungarian Empire, but the construction of the Municipal House was by the order of the City Hall, where a Czech patriotic atmosphere was already prevalent. It is no coincidence that, several years after the building's completion, the independent Czechoslovak Republic was declared in the Municipal House.
Despite its indisputable social and political importance, Smetana Hall is devoted mainly to classical music, linked mainly to the prodigious work of Bedřich Smetana (1824–1884). Since the end of the Second World War the music festival "Prague Spring" annually takes place in this refined hall. It is always opened with Smetana's important piece of work – symphonic poem "My Country" – interpreted by leading Czech or foreign musicians. Besides this, other world-renowned compositions, pieces, and overtures of Smetana's famous operas, such as "The Bartered Bride", "Dalibor", "The Secret", and "The Devil's Wall". The fact that the name of this composer was linked to the music hall became a shield which protected the Municipal House from the malevolence of the communist regime in the 1950s, when they considered tearing it down as an inappropriate symbol of the "old" times.

374 < František Hergesel, medallion of Bedřich Smetana on the organ
375 > Rows of folding seats in the auditorium

376 < View of hall from the main balcony during a concert

> 377

> 378

> 379

377 < Wainscoting of the proscenium

378 < Detail of the draperies

379 < Decoration of the railing above the proscenium

380 > Railing on the steps in front of the organ, detail

381 > Suspension of one of the six hanging lights above the proscenium, originally equipped with arc lamps

382 > Detail of the railing above the proscenium by the organ

> 380

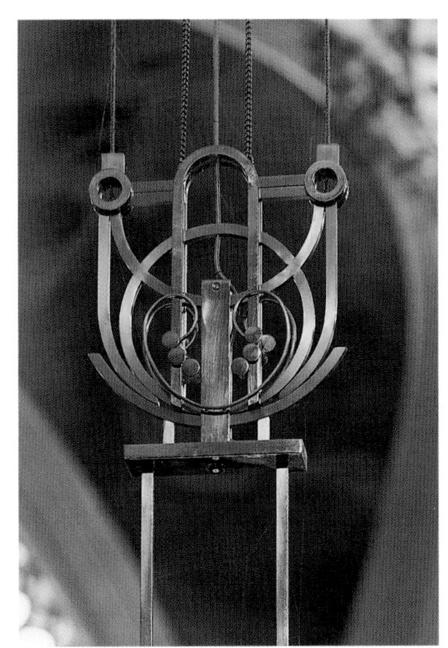

> 381

> 382

383 > Lighting unit on the organ
384 –385 > Organ, details
386 > Decoration of the pillar on the main balcony

> 383

> 384

> 385

> 386

> 387

387 << View of the base of a vault at the rear of the hall, with lighting under the parapet of the main balcony
388 << Top part of a pillar with a decorative sculpture by Karel Novák and a detail of the decoration of the walls and ceiling

389 > View of the hall from the gallery of the proscenium during an orchestra rehearsal
390 > View of the hall from the main balcony during an orchestra rehearsal

> 389

> 390

> 391

> 392

391 < Ceiling with stripes of lights
392 < Ceiling with roof light, detail
393 > Decoration of a balcony parapet, detail

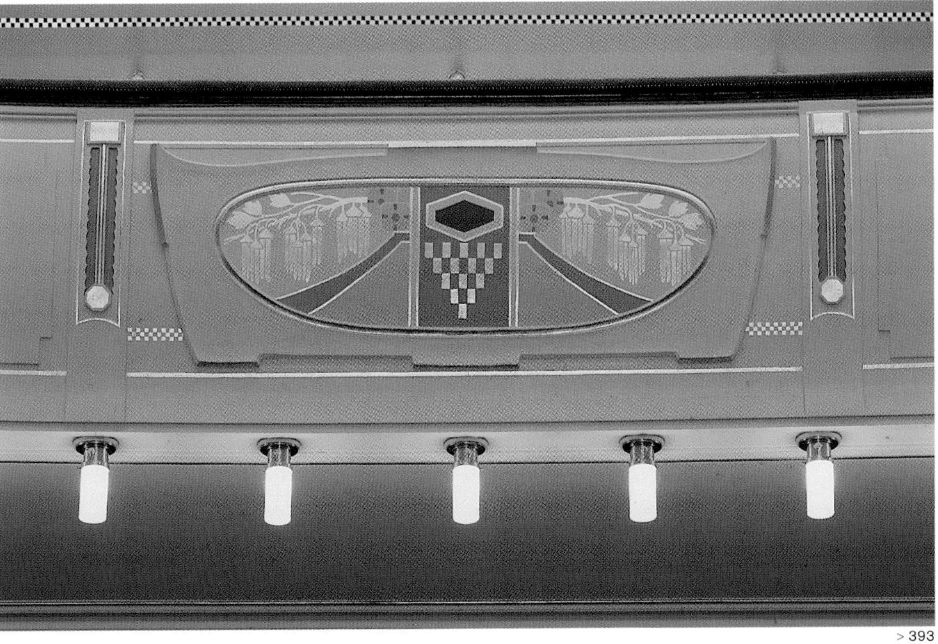

> 393

> 395

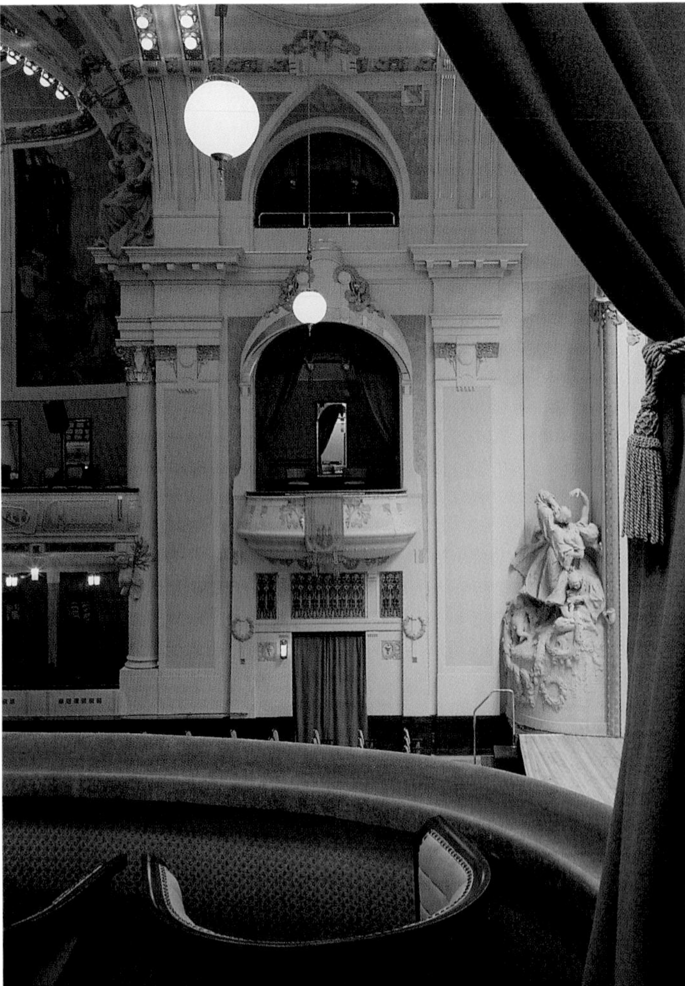

> 396

394 << View of the side wall of the hall with balconies and murals by Karel Špillar

395 > Parapet of the president's box

396 > View of the hall when looking from the mayor's box to the president's box

397 > Main balcony

> 398

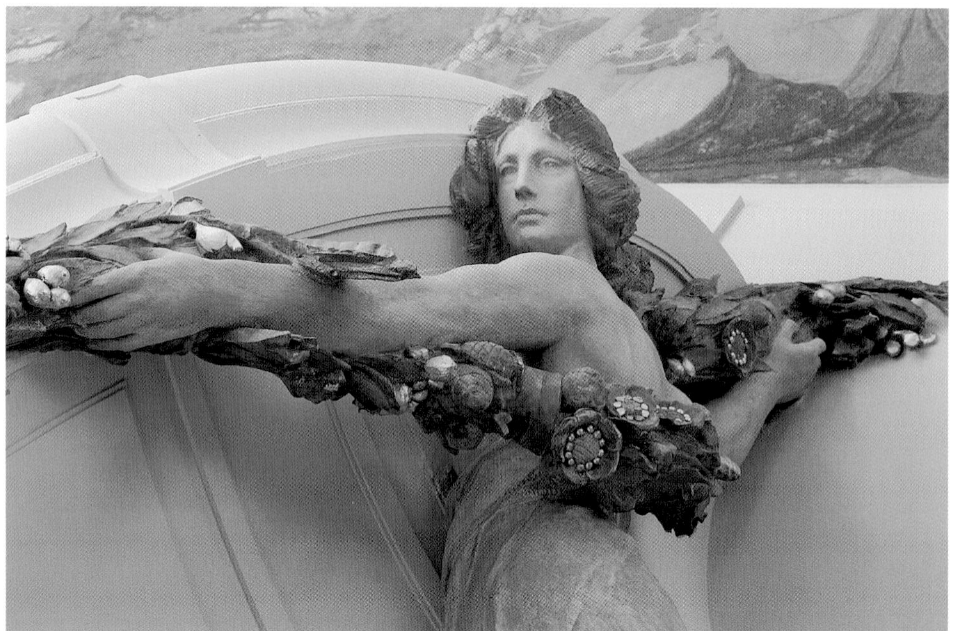

> 399

398–399 < Figural decoration of the hall, details
400–401 > Ladislav Šaloun, Vyšehrad, details
402 > Ladislav Šaloun, Slavonic Dances, detail

> 400

> 401

> 402

> 403

> 404

403 > Ladislav Šaloun, Slavonic Dances

404 > Detail of a top side balcony and a mural by Karel Špillar

405 > A view of main balcony from a side top balcony

> 406

406 < Ceiling of the hall with stained-glass panes and allegorical paintings by Karel Špillar

> 407

407 < View of the boxes on the side of the hall
408 > Stripe of ceiling lights, detail
409 > Emergency lighting, detail
410 > Air-vent grill, detail

> 408

> 409

> 410

411 > Entrance to the main balcony from the second-floor foyer
412 > Side entrance into the hall
413 > View of the entrance from the second-floor foyer
414 > View of a side entrance from the first-floor corridor

> 411

> 412

> 413

> 414

> 415

415 < Glass wall into the first-floor foyer
416 > New parlor for an orchestra conductor
in the former serving room of the Confectionery

> 416

Oriental Parlor

This parlor was originally called the Serbian Parlor and it belongs to the "ladies' parlors" of the first floor. Its decoration draws inspiration from Islamic-Anatolian art, seen particularly on the walls and in decorative elements. The orientation towards eastern cultures corresponded with the forsaking of the Germanic culture of central Europe, and also exhibited an interest in the "Orient" that was quite fashionable at the beginning of the 20th century. The strikingly colorful décor and east-inspired filigree workmanship were a great foundation for the presentation of the "golden Czech hands", the Czech arts and crafts, which at that time surpassed the "German" polished Prague interiors.

The richly adorned ceiling is decorated with eye-catching, multi-colored geometric designs, incorporating gilding and painted glass lenses and rectangles. The center segment is embellished with three ovals, which are intersected by a rectangular frame of a stucco meander pattern. The smaller segments thus created are decorated with spirals and wrought-brass rosettes, from which four lighting units spring. The lighting units are made of wrought-brass sheet embellished with "helmets", colored glass inserts, glass cylinders, and pendants.

The perimeter of the ceiling is defined by a carved wooden frame, which also borders the side sections of the ceiling. These sections are decorated with rhomboids and rosettes, into which round brass lighting units with glass covers are fitted.

The walls are articulated by intersecting arcs, flanked with stucco molding that is inlaid with colorful glass lenses. The spandrels are decorated with stucco mosaic. The concave segments between the arcades are embellished with decorative painting. The hanging covering the doorway to Grégr Hall features the same pattern. The walls are completed with finely wrought brass air vent grills, which can be manipulated by chains. The lower part of the parlor is wainscoted with light ash wood. The built-in furniture is richly carved.

The door leading from the corridor is decorated with clear, beveled glass panels in brass frames and with sunken rectangular ornamental wooden panels. Four arcs and rosettes in the panel above the door serve to incorporate it into the parlor's decoration. Alongside the door are stacked cabinets with glass-covered tops, and upholstered corner seating units that are linked to the wainscoting. Corner banquettes are completed with embroidered cushions and appliqués. The parlor is further complemented with polygonal tables with inlaid tops, a radiator cover under the window, and a set of extendable tables. The textile drapes with fringes and the sheer curtains were made according to period photographs.

> 418

> 419

> 420

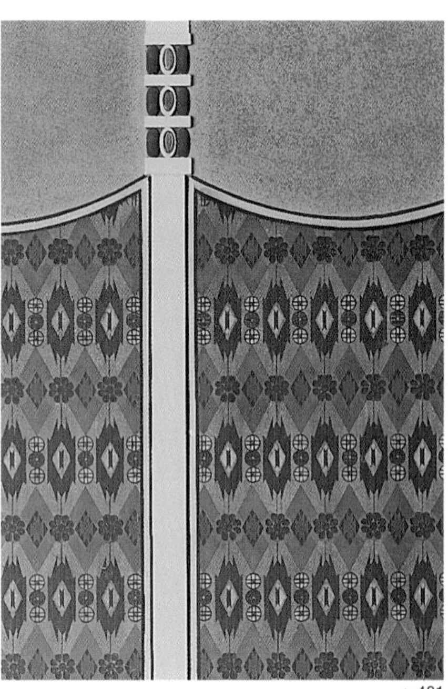

> 421

417 <<< View of the window wall

418 << View of the entrance to Grégr Hall

419 < Built-in table in front of the window, detail
420 < Serving tables, detail
421 < Ornamental painting on the walls, detail
422 > Grill of the radiator cover, detail
423 > Top part of the bench back, detail
424 > Hand rest of a seat, detail

> 422

> 423

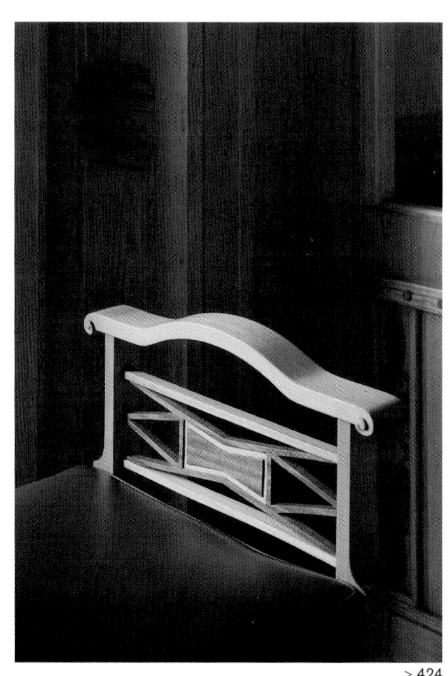

> 424

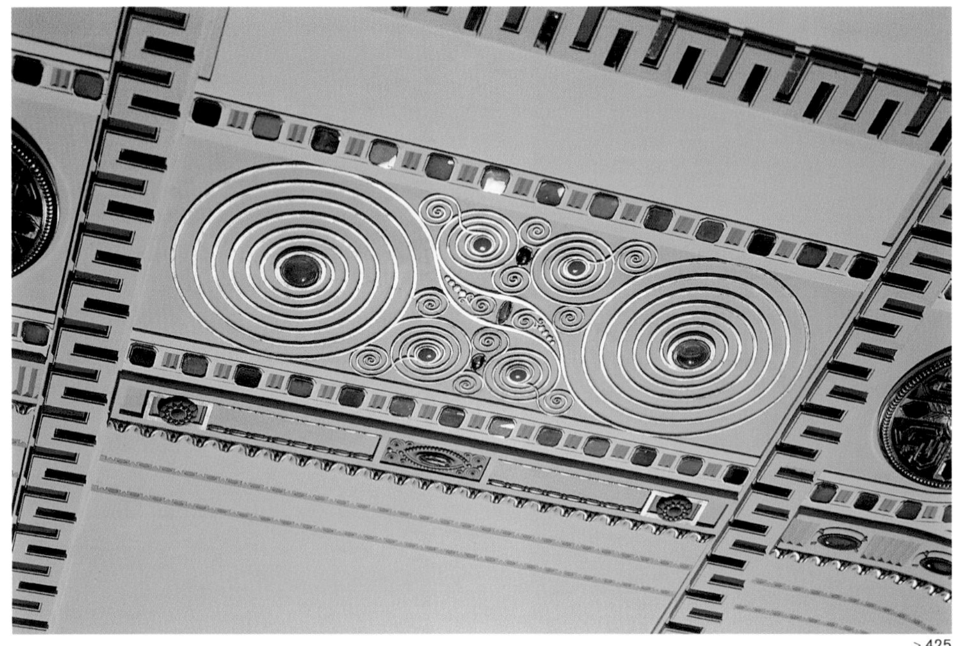

> 425

> 426

425 < Ceiling decoration, detail
426 < Ceiling lighting unit
427 > Chandelier and a detail of the wall decoration with a vent grill

> 427

> 428

428 < Built-in bench with a table

429 > View of the Božena Němcová Parlor from the Oriental Parlor

> 429

Božena Němcová Parlor

This parlor is located in the bend of the first floor, between the Oriental and the Moravian Slovakian Parlors. The word parlor, meaning a small room, is quite apt to describe this tiny room, left in an irregular corner of the floor plan. This is why subtle decoration was chosen and the parlor was symbolically dedicated to a female writer – Božena Němcová.

The most striking feature of the room is the mosaic in the fountain niche, made of colored pieces of glass, arranged in radiating decorative bands. The fountain shell is made of white marble, inserted in a red marble socle. The space between the shell and the socle is decorated with plants. The plants and water evoke tenderness and refreshing female grace. The cascade fountain is made of burned-clay blocks and consists of a socle, side columns, and a small entablature, on which rests a small majolica sculpture of the writer. In the central part of the fountain, a wrought brass bowl is inserted. The walls of the room are wainscoted with light artificial marble, which is vertically articulated. Above the niche archivolt and above the artificial marble, a decorative multi-color and gilded molding stretches around the entire room. On the ceiling, there is a polychrome stucco frame around an oval centerpiece with two circular medallions. The window wall is decorated with curtains, designed according to period photographs, and a tabernacle radiator cover of patina-coated bronze. The cover is finely wrought, and showcases a planter in the white marble. In the corners next to the window, there are two banquettes with light-colored upholstery, which make it possible for a visitor to take an intimate break in this otherwise palatial building. The parquet floor contains an oval motif, inlaid as though embroidered.

Without any doors, this triangular room cleverly links the adjacent halls of similar decoration. The cozy interior incites one to contemplate and remember the progressive woman of the 19th century, for whom the parlor was named. Božena Němcová (1820–1862) was not only a narrator of Czech and Slovak fairy tales, but she also masterfully captured rural and urban life in a broad social context, emphasizing the undignified status and hard life of the women of the time. Her most important piece of work is "Grandmother" ("Babička"), a novel consisting of "pictures of the country life". Nowadays, Božena Němcová is considered an important representative of Czech national literature and a symbol of modern feminism. The "slender" space of this parlor corresponds with the impressive grace of this woman and is as important to the Municipal House as the more spacious parlors named after important men of the nation.

> 430

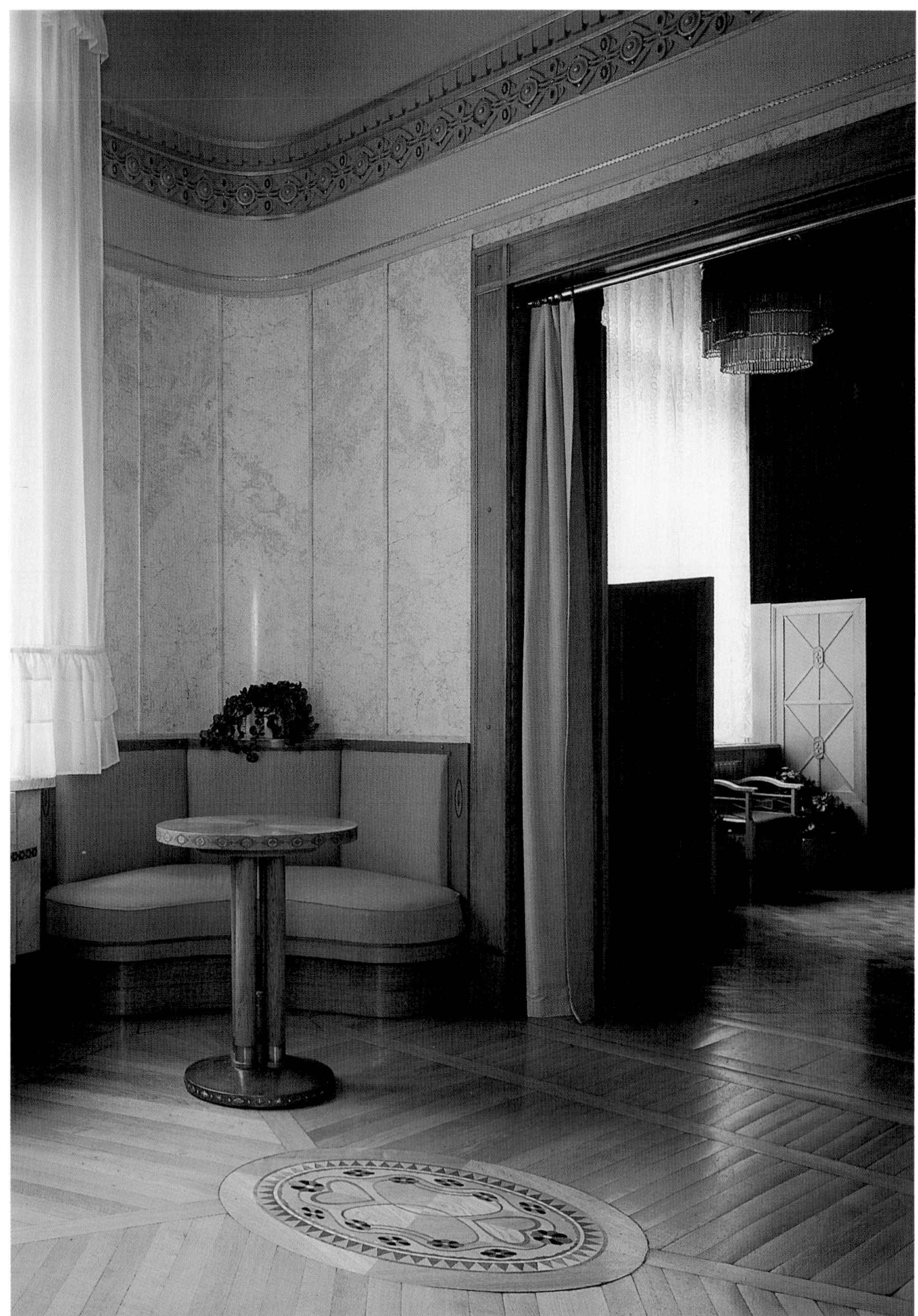

> 431

430 << Ceramic fountain in a niche with a sculpture of the writer

431 > Corner seating unit with a table and inlaid floor
432 > Ceiling decoration, detail
433 > Table, detail of the base
434 > Table, detail of the top

> 432

> 433

> 434

435–437 > Fountain and niche mosaic, details

438 > Fountain, detail of the central part

> 435

> 436

> 437

> 439

> 440

> 441

439 < Ornamental band on the wall, detail
440 < Air vent grill
441 < Floor inlay, detail
442 > Radiator cover, detail

> 442

Moravian Slovakian Parlor

Among the "ladies' parlors", this one is distinguished by its simple and subdued colors. Upon entering, the visitor is charmed by a welcoming atmosphere, reminiscent of a grandmother's parlor. That is due in part to an aquarium with aquatic plants and fish, but mainly to the canvas embroidery, macramé curtains, furs, furniture, and parquet floor.

The square ceiling is bordered with a band divided into rectangles, with gilded and polychrome stucco folk motifs, that runs along the walls just below the ceiling. However, the overall impression of a civil apartment rather than a luxurious palace is preserved. Similar motifs embellish an indented round ceiling centerpiece, which evokes for visitors an intimate home-like atmosphere. It is set in a fillet frame, which stretches along diagonal lines into medallions, from which descend brass chandeliers with glass lusters. The inner surface of the ceiling centerpiece is filled with simple painted lace.

Along the walls of the Moravian Slovakian Parlor are fitted comfortable banquettes with leather upholstery and a top band "warmed" with white fur. The wall above the banquettes is simply articulated by fillet frames into rectangles with oval mirrors. The bordering wooden molding that links the austere walls with the ornate ceiling is decorated with billets. The walls are covered with wallpaper. The large room is articulated by wooden portals of light ash wood ornamented with rounded fronts and carving. Rustic embroidered lambrequins, with macramé with beads and squares, hang between them.

A wooden socle with a post carrying a unique, stacked brass fish tank with sculpted motifs of snails is attached to the wall with the entrance to the Božena Němcová Parlor. The furniture further consists of polygonal tables with green marble tops. Along their perimeters, they are embellished with delicate carving, and they stand on a single pedestal. Fully upholstered, horseshoe-shaped armchairs and banquettes comprise the majority of the seating furniture.

Incorporated in the window composition is a wooden radiator cover, decorated with brass grill and plant containers, indispensable for this type of interior.

> 444

443 << View from the passage from the Božena Němcová Parlor

444 < View of the parlor from the corridor
445 > Crystal chandelier
446 > Armchairs and a table, detail

447 >> View of the parlor when looking towards the door
to the Confectionery

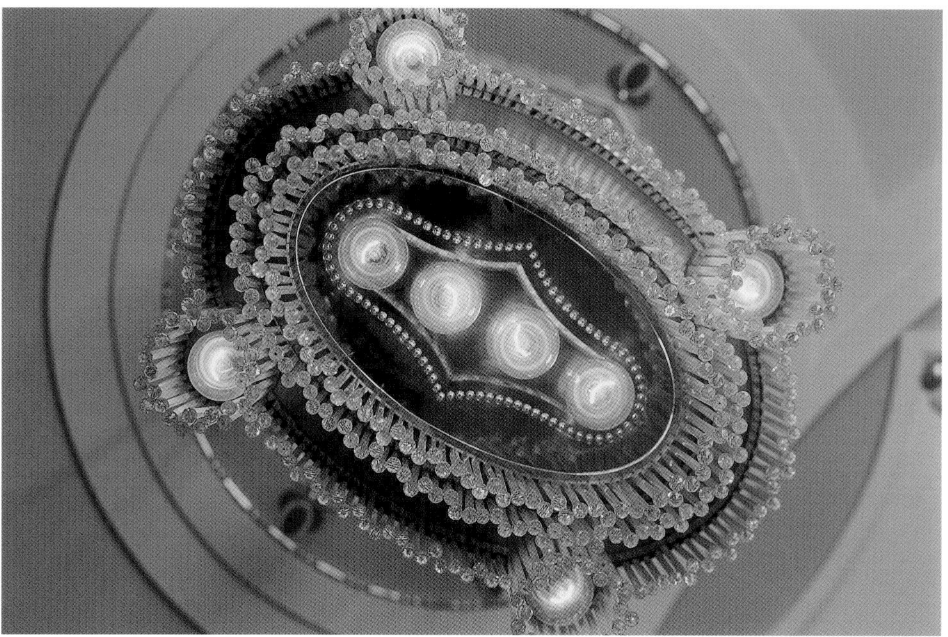

> 445

> 446

> 448

> 449

> 450

448 < Aquarium
449 < Aquarium, detail with a snail-shaped gargoyle
450 < Door hanging, detail of embroidery
451 > Chandelier with lusters, detail
452 > Ceiling decoration, detail
453 > Seating unit, detail

> 451

> 452

> 453

454–455 > Embroidered hangings above the door, details
456 > Embroidered and macramé hangings

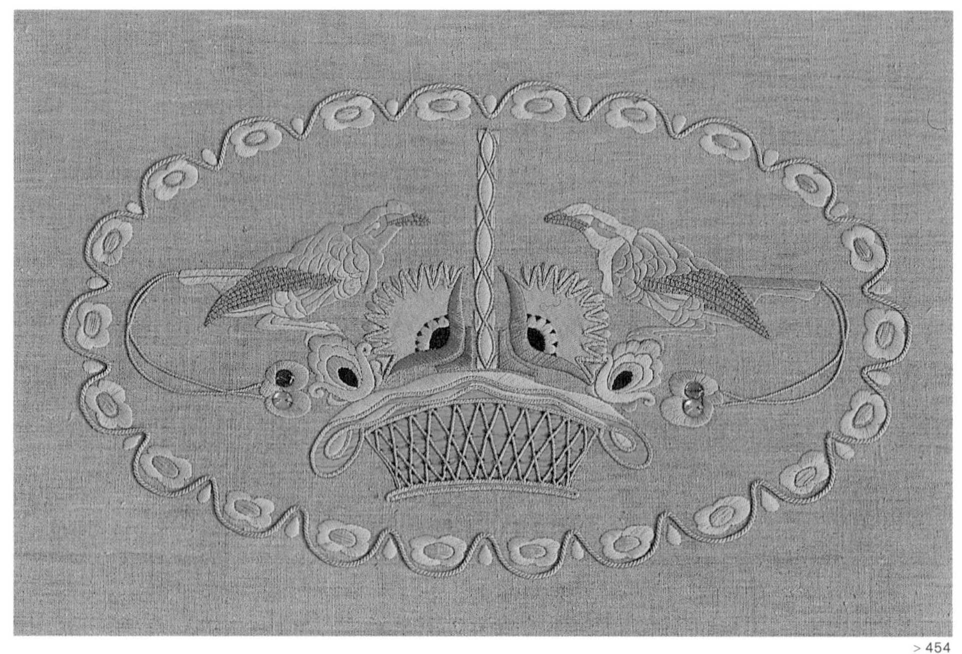

> 454

> 455

> 456

> 457

457 < Window wall
458 > Macramé hangings by the side door
459 > View of the Confectionery

> 458

> 459

Confectionery

The largest of the "ladies' parlors" is the "Confectionery", which is of a neo-classicist character with Art-Nouveau features. As is clear from the name and the purpose, it is a pleasant, "sweet-toned" room in light hues, however, strongly over-decorated like a typical Viennese cake. The comparison to a cake is perhaps slightly simplistic, but it captures the design concept of the Confectionery as compared to the other halls of the Municipal House.

The room's main feature is the elaborate stucco decoration of the ceiling and walls, with striking gilding on a white background. The basic ceiling structure is in three parts, linked to the vertical articulation of the walls by pilasters, and by the pillars of the portal into the adjacent room. The central part of the ceiling has an oval stucco centerpiece set in a square frame with indented corners. The side segments are separated in three parts by bands. Each central one is again ornate with an oval centerpiece and the side ones with rhomboid shapes. Under the ceiling, decorative molding stretches around the room, connecting the zoomorphic pilaster capitals and adding new ornate features to the stucco decoration of the room.

The walls are wainscoted with white artificial marble and embellished with large mirrors composed of smaller rectangles. The radiator covers, also made of white marble, have ornate brass grills. Upholstered sofas with fluted and carved headboards are built into the bottom part of the walls made of light maple wood. An original supplement to the sofas are brass candelabra lights, topped with motifs of stylized palm trees.

The composition of the frontal wall behind the bar begins with axially positioned mirrored doors, between showcases and brass three-arm candelabras. A glass panel, decorated with garlands of bulbs, is situated above the door. The space above this set is dominated by a rectangular stucco relief of two kneeling female figures and a garland, which is set in a wide glass mirror frame broken up into smaller segments.

The corners of the front wall are dominated by two glass-panel cabinets. The refreshment bar with white marble top and two pastry cases with beveled glass panes belong to the same set. All of the interior furniture was made of light maple, but the originally white hues had turned yellow and brown over the many years of use (and maintenance). As part of a challenging renovation in 1996, all the wooden elements were taken apart, whitened, and newly lacquered.

In the adjacent room there is a picture by Václav Jansa called "Tábor". The portal of the entrance into the Moravian Slovakian Parlor is covered with artificial marble with gilded decorative elements and topped with a zoomorphic composition around an urn. The main ceiling chandeliers, circular in shape with candlesticks fitted around the circumference, hang down on brass bars and glass chains. Small lighting units with long glass lusters and wall-fitted cascade brass lights complete the illumination of the room.

The Confectionery's movable furniture consists of round tables with white marble tops, gilded, profiled table bases, and period light-colored chairs with cane strapping. Textile draperies and curtains, made according to period photographs, complete the window wall.

The door behind the bar originally served to connect the Confectionery with the serving and preparation rooms, but is now blocked because the original serving room has been changed into a conductor's parlor.

The connecting corridor outside the "ladies' parlors" has a flat ceiling with emphasized entrances into the boxes of Smetana Hall and into the Confectionery. The ceiling of this section, articulated with basket-shaped arch rings, is ornate with a fillet frame with conches, mascarons and musical emblems (a lyre).

The opposite wall of the box entrances, including the pillar, is wainscoted with light green artificial marble. The entrance into the Confectionery, embellished with a segmented fanlight, is filled with beveled glass set in brass frames in the shapes of scalloped edges, stones, and jewel-cut glass. The corridor walls have wood wainscoting filled with wallpaper. The entrance doors into the Moravian Slovakian Parlor and the Oriental Parlor also consist of small, beveled, clear and colored glass panes. The names of the parlors are inscribed in the door pediments. The opposite wall has the same decoration with a built-in upholstered sofa and a mirror.

And so an independent promenade was formed in front of the Confectionery, allowing a dignified link to the other halls of the Municipal House independent of adjoining halls.

> 460

460 << Interior with a seating unit

461 > Frontal wall with a bar and glass-panel cabinets
462 > View of the room towards the Moravian Slovakian Parlor

> 461

> 462

> 463

> 464

> 465

463 < Radiator cover, detail
464 < Chairs and table, detail
465 < Detail of a door
466 > Table, detail of the base
467 > Pastry case, detail
468 > Glass decoration above the entrance from the corridor

> 466

> 467

> 468

> 469

469 < Chandeliers and the frontal wall decoration

470 > View of the sculptures above the entrance to the Moravian Slovakian Parlor

471 > Frontal wall, detail of decoration

472 > Side mirror wall with an air vent grill and a light, detail

> 470

> 471

> 472

473 > View of hall with the frontal wall and a bar

> 474

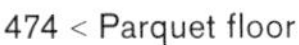

474 < Parquet floor

475 > Decoration of the walls and ceiling, detail

> 475

> 476

> 477

476 < View of the bar and a glass-panel cabinet in the front of the Confectionery

477 > Sculptures above the door to the Moravian Slovakian Parlor

> 478

> 479

> 480

478 < Back part of the Confectionery separated by columns with a painting of Tábor by Václav Jansa and a door to the Moravian Slovakian Parlor

479 > View of the Confectionery from the Moravian Slovakian Parlor

480 > Main entrance from the corridor

Dining Parlors

A row of parlors of the north wing, located along the outer side of the sharply turned corridor past Sladkovský Hall, is designed as a set of "dining parlors". These five parlors are without permanent furnishing, so that the interiors can be varied according to the needs of the moment. They are usually used for official receptions and exhibition openings, as well as for small exhibitions and presentations. The parlors can be used individually or they can be linked by opening the partition walls.

The ceilings of the original four dining parlors are articulated into striking geometrical compositions and support brass lighting units that were designed in a style to complement to the Art-Nouveau interior.

Another interesting feature is the sliding partition doors, in which brass frames, formed in geometrical Art-Nouveau shapes hold beveled clear-glass panes. The walls above the wooden wainscoting of dark-stained oak were covered with new wallpaper bearing a large-shape pattern, copied from the original that was found in one of the dining parlors. All of the parlors are decorated with the same pattern of wallpaper, which produces a silk effect, but each individual room has its own color.

An important part of the panels in the wainscoting of the west dining parlor is a wall-mounted beveled mirror with a typical Art-Nouveau decorative frame – of a segmented arch and a circle – completed with a clock on a cantilever. The wall-mounted mirror in the east dining parlor is similarly articulated by a large circle, above which there is a brass clock. The former serving room, adjoining the east dining parlor, was newly altered into another parlor in the same style. It is decorated with a painting by Adolf Liebscher called "Český Krumlov".

The drapes covering large windows are newly designed to complement curtains with a pattern similar to the one on the wallpaper.

The connecting corridor outside the dining parlors, with the one obvious exception of the entrance niche into the boxes of Smetana Hall, is designed in an austere fashion. The linear centerpieces of the ceiling segments have similar moldings stretching to the walls. Spherical lights in brass frames are fitted in the ceiling segments. The emphasized central part of the corridor is decorated with a layered centerpiece, archivolt openings with ornate lesenes, and round medallions with the profiles of girls' faces in the bases of the ceiling molds.

Wooden entrances into the dining parlors, with wide double doors, have beveled glass panels set in brass frames, creating vertical geometrical bands. The segmented fanlight is embellished with rich stained glass and a central oval with the inscription "DINING PARLORS". Besides the four doors leading into the dining parlors, the corridor is decorated with a single mirror in a wooden frame and a three-part mirror with a small canopy and built-in lights.

> 482

481 << View of the frontal wall of the west dining parlor, with a mirror and a clock

482 < Frontal wall of the west dining parlor, with a mirror and a clock, detail
483 > View of the door separating the east Dining Parlor
484 > View of the large dining parlor when looking to the west

485 >> View of the east dining parlors when looking from the west one

> 483

> 484

> 486

> 487

> 488

486–488 < Glass panes in the dining parlors doors, details
489 > Entrance door from the corridor into the large dining parlor

> 489

Czech Club

Since the opening of the Municipal House, this room became a center of rich club and political life, which fulfilled the creators' intentions of establishing a multi-purpose ceremonial building. However, not even the most zealous patriots could predict that in this building an independent Czechoslovak Republic would be declared.

These rooms, already in use during the First World War by Czech representatives and political parties, gained the name of the Czech Club. Some rooms were used by the Agrarian Party (Agrarian Club), others by the English and the Gentlemen's Clubs. In July 1918, the National Committee was established here, and eventually it was allowed to use the space of the Gentlemen's Club. At the suggestion of František Soukup, a marble plaque commemorating the men of October 28 was made. The plaque was made by Vlastislav Hofman and the portraits by Josef Šejnost. Besides the portraits of František Soukup, Alois Rašín, Antonín Švehla, Jiří Stříbrný and Vavro Šrobár, there is also the following text written by a historian Josef Pekař:

"THIS ROOM WITNESSED THE MAKING OF HISTORY, IN THIS ROOM THE NATIONAL COMMITTEE, AWAITING THE FALL OF THE AUSTRIAN EMPIRE AND PREPARING FOR CZECH LIBERATION, HELD ITS MEETINGS. IN THIS ROOM, ON THE TRIUMPHANT DAY OF OCTOBER 28, 1918, THE COMMITTEE TOOK OVER THE POWER OF THE CZECH LANDS, IN THIS ROOM THE WORDS OF COMENIUS WERE FULFILLED: 'THE RULE OVER YOUR MATTERS SHALL RETURN TO YOU, CZECH PEOPLE.'"

In the next room a plaque commemorating handing the military power over to the National Committee was fitted:

"IN THIS HALL OF THE CZECH GENTLEMEN'S CLUB, WHERE CZECH WILL, CZECH SUFFERING, CZECH DEFIANCE, AND CZECH BELIEF HAVE BEEN EXPRESSED IN A FRIENDLY CONCORD FROM THE FIRST DAY OF THE WORLD WAR, BETWEEN THE EVENING HOURS OF 8 AND 9 O'CLOCK THE FORMER AUSTRIAN MILITARY POWER OF THE 8TH ARMY CORPS WAS HANDED OVER TO THE NATIONAL COMMITTEE."

The reversals of Czech history were reflected in the fate of the commemorative plaques. At the order of Protectorate officials, all Czech inscriptions in the Municipal House had to be removed, thus both commemorative plaques were taken down on June 21, 1940.

The plaques were forgotten for many years. They were, after being repaired, put in their places during the renovation of the Municipal House in 1997.

Before the First World War, the club rooms were furnished with movables designed by Josef Chochol, one of the most famous authors fulfilling ideas of a specifically Czech architectural style – Cubism – in the world-wide context. The club rooms, already decorated in this modern style in 1912, shortly after the completion of the Municipal House construction, belonged among the earliest examples of Cubist interiors in Prague. The original appearance is preserved in period photographs and in a drawing by J. Skrbek in the Museum of the City of Prague. The documentation as well as the preserved original pieces of the furnishing, which are now a part of the collections of the Museum of Decorative Arts in Prague, are proof of the high value of Chochol's design. They are sometimes exhibited even abroad. Brought together in these interiors is an overview of the different phases of the Prague Art-Nouveau style that can be seen in the Municipal House.

> 490

490 << Cubist seating unit, detail

491 < View of the wall with a panel and plaques commemorating the men of October 28 by Josef Šejnost

> 492

> 493

> 494

492–494 < Cubist furniture

495–498 > Cubist furniture, details

> 495

> 496

> 497

> 498

Second-Floor Foyer

One can get to the foyer outside the Exhibition Halls via the shoulders of the main stairway. They lead upwards from the central foyer outside Smetana Hall and continue on both sides to landings with portals of crimson artificial marble panels. Each of these large landings is decorated by two female half-figures with draperies, wreaths, and garlands with ribbons, all in gilded stucco.

The entrance into the main exhibition hall is through the second-floor foyer, which opens into the main corridor, situated in the same way as the corridors and foyer on the first floor. However, the balcony of Smetana Hall enroaches on the space and overall size of the second-floor foyer, and can be entered through three swing doors and up several wooden steps. Despite the smaller size, the foyer is still spacious and, together with the corridor, lighted through the glass ceiling; it allows for the expansion of exhibitions into this part of the building. The foyer is decorated and articulated with two columns with Art-Nouveau composite capitals.

The ceiling of the perimeter wall is segmented, with inserted glass panels, which are, in turn, covered with glass roof-lights. The major decoration of the entrance into the central Hollar Exhibition Hall is the arch of the portal, flanked by a flat band and white marble steps. The double door is filled with beveled glass panels.

> 500

499 << View of the corridor outside the exhibition halls

500 < View of the foyer from the main stairway, with an elevator shaft with decorative grill
501 > View of the entrances to Smetana Hall balcony from the entrance to the Hollar Hall
502 > Sculptures outside the entrance to Smetana Hall, detail

> 501

> 502

503 > Sconce supplied by the František Křižík firm on the pillar of the elevator shaft on the main stairway
504 > Lighting unit on the foyer ceiling
505 > Emergency lighting
506 > View of a sconce and the glass-paneled ceiling above the main stairway

> 503

> 504

> 505

> 506

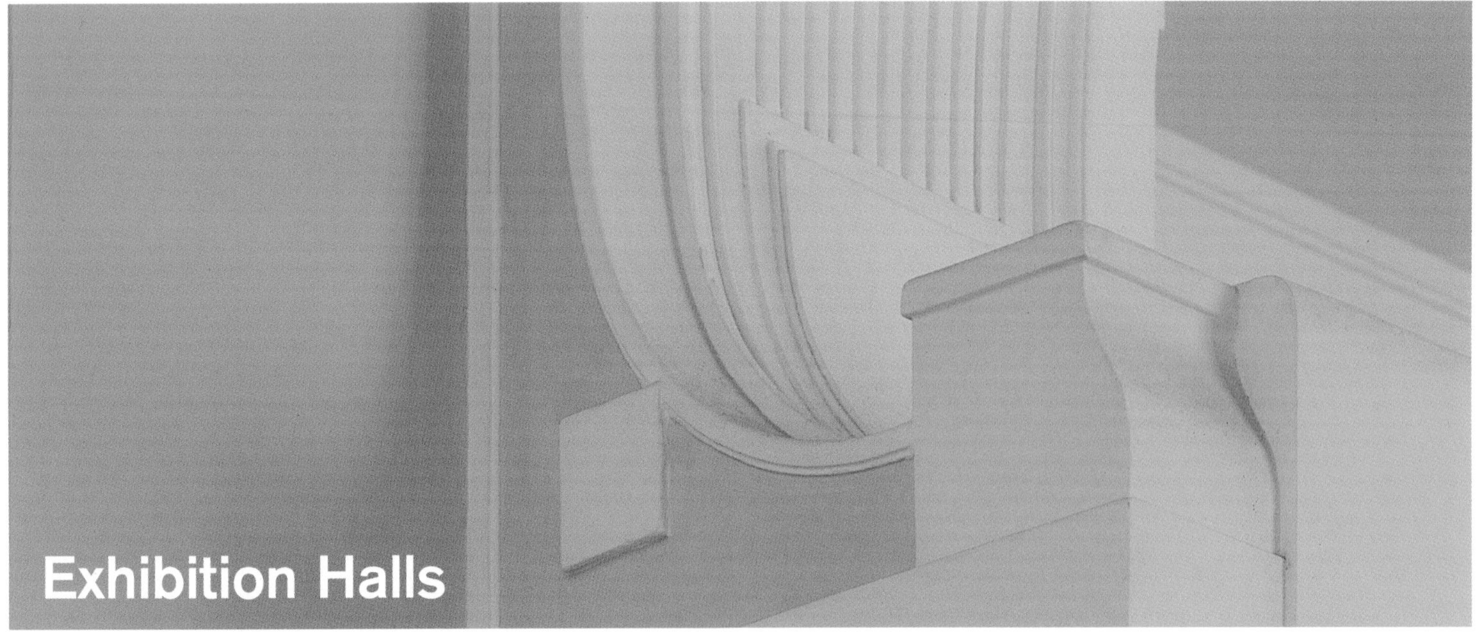

Exhibition Halls

The unique rooms of the "Exhibition Halls", designed mainly for large exhibitions, are lighted with soft diffused light coming though the glass double ceiling, which is particularly suitable for the presentation of sculpture. That is probably why the exhibition of the renowned Auguste Rodin's sculptures, organized shortly after the opening of this building, had such a striking and emotional impact on the Czech public. However, these halls are also well-designed for the exhibition of paintings, and there is even a special raised section for exhibiting small artifacts (originally designed for goldsmiths and numismatists). During the reconstruction at the end of the 20th century, these high-quality exhibition halls, located in the roof space, were outfitted with an electronic alarm system.

Hollar Hall, the round central entrance hall, was named after a world-famous Czech graphic artist and engraver of the 17th century, Václav Hollar.

In the center of the hall is a glass-paneled dome, articulated with high entablature at its springing line and decorated along the vertical lesenes with classicist wreaths with ribbons. The walls are articulated with niches with marble sills and conches filled with wrought grills.

Both rectangular exhibition halls, lighted by the aforementioned rooflights, are vaulted with high cavetto moldings. An eye-catching feature of the left hall is an arcade, situated in the long axis. It creates an entrance into the raised room, a platform of a sort, in the north bay. The entrance itself is designed as a Moorish arch with decorated entablature and two pairs of Tuscan columns and pilasters. The bottom part of the archivolt is fluted; the top is decorated with a cartouche with Art-Nouveau acanthus molding.

The right exhibition hall was left without any striking architectural elements or further articulation, and so the large ceiling with glass panels and softly rounded ceiling corners stands out. Both main halls have efficiently designed entrances from the central circular exhibition hall. However, if need be, a series of double doors leading to the adjacent corridor can be used.

Events organized in the timeless exhibition halls were, and still are, an expression of a new stage in the modern Czech way of perceiving and contemplating the visual arts and architecture, as well as a general feeling for style. It was first expressed in the opening exhibition on January 5, 1912, installed by architect Pavel Janák, presenting Cubist paintings, furniture, and arts and crafts, or also in an exhibition arranged by Josef Gočár, highlighting, among others, the works of Pablo Picasso and Georges Braque.

Today's management of the Municipal House is continuing the important tradition by organizing exhibitions of works of foreign as well as Czech personalities, who, in a significant way, determined and determine the evolution of the production of art.

> 508

507 << Hollar Hall

508 < View of the left, north exhibition hall from the Hollar Hall
509 > Ceiling of Hollar Hall
510 > Decoration of the wall in Hollar Hall wall, detail

> 509

> 510

> 511

> 512

> 513

511–513 > Exhibitions in exhibition halls

514 > View of the left exhibition hall from the platform in the north bay

> 514

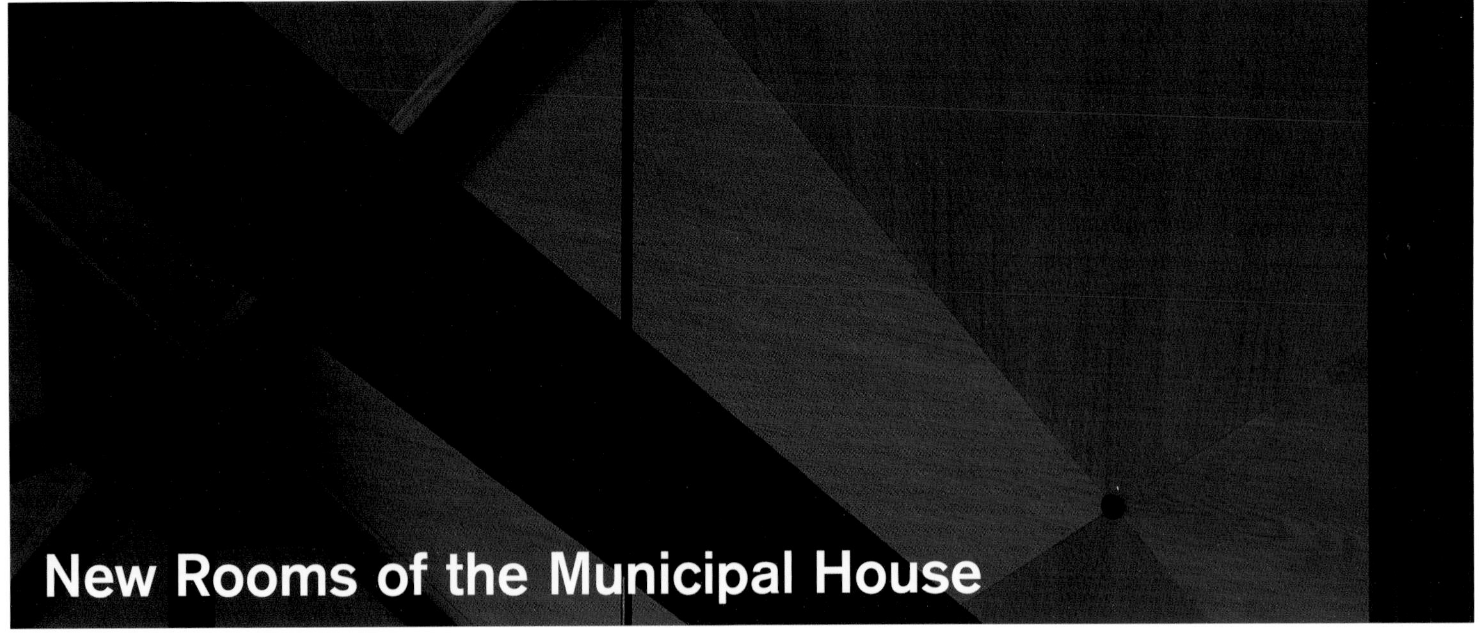

New Rooms of the Municipal House

The Orchestra Conductor's Apartment > High in the attic, above the Smetana Hall stage, a spacious Orchestra Conductor's Apartment was newly designed. It is dominated by a large semicircular window, which is geometrically articulated and placed in the axis above the corner tower. It provides a wonderful view of the silhouette of the Týn church, the Old Town roofs and the still impressive panorama of Prague.

The interior was designed in terra cotta and brown colors and it is completed by a folding wall, which conceals a bed and bathroom. The parquet floor has geometrical articulation into stripes. The exposed steel structure of the roof beams of the Municipal House transports the contemporary perception to the turn of the 19th and 20th centuries because it reminds one of daring riveted constructions such as the Eiffel Tower in Paris.

Cultural and Information Center > Under the Central Cloakroom, in the former furniture storage room, a new Cultural and Information Center was built. For visitors to the Municipal House, it represents a much needed base as well as the starting point for tours of the building.

The entrance into this relatively spacious room is through a narrow passageway along the left side of the main stairway in the ground-floor foyer. Both the floor and the walls of the room were designed in blue, which is completed by the silver color of the modern furniture and the light wood of the store and bar counters.

The center, which also contains a small café, offers information about cultural events in the Municipal House. In addition to tickets for cultural events, visitors can buy books, Art-Nouveau objects, and souvenirs as a permanent reminder of this unique Art-Nouveau building in the very heart of Prague.

515 > Stairway to the Orchestra Conductor's Apartment

516 > Orchestra Conductor's Apartment

> 515

> 516

> 517

> 518

517 < View of the Old Town and Prague Castle from the Orchestra Conductor's Apartment
518 < Orchestra Conductor's Apartment with the original steel structure of the roof beams
519 > Cultural and Information Center

> 519

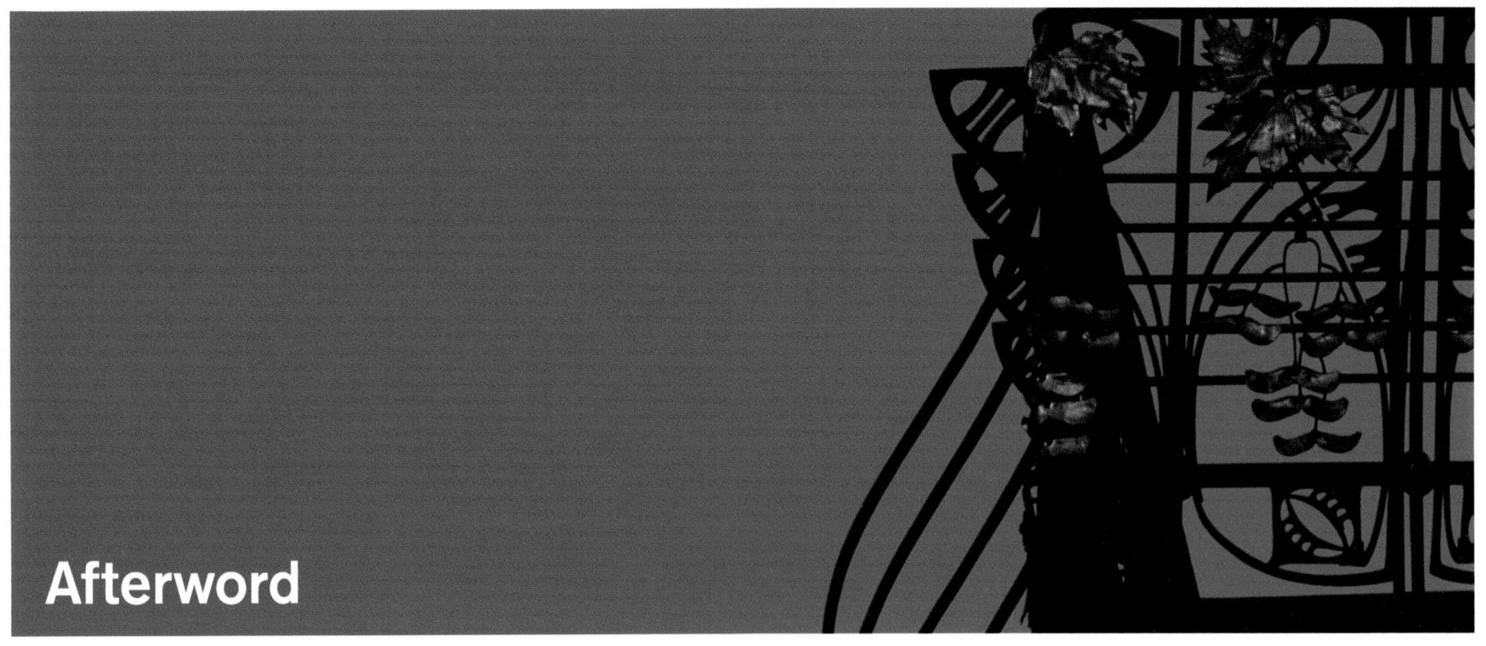

Afterword

Dear readers,
and so this ends the tour of the Municipal House in this publication. Even an extensive book such as this one can cover only a part of the artistic treasures of the Municipal House, and one visit of the representative areas of this Art-Nouveau jewel can hardly be enough for anyone to take in all of its aesthetic qualities.
In comparison with other Prague monuments, the Municipal House has an exceptional character: it shows visitors not only the beauty of the past, but its hospitality provides singular cultural experiences through numerous cultural activities.
The person seeking to learn more about the Czech nation and to better know its civic community will find more than one answer to his questions in the Municipal House.

Dear guests, undoubtedly on each successive visit you will find new decorative motifs, you will notice other details, and you will be attracted by new specialties, which together form the unique artistic whole of the Municipal House. During each further visit you will appreciate the great foresight, resourcefulness, and talents of preceding generations. We are trying to preserve the results of their artistic and artisanal works placed into our care, so that during your later stays in Prague your steps will once again lead to the Municipal House of the city of Prague.

František Laudát > Director of the Municipal House

> 520

520 << View of the left wing of the Municipal House and the Powder Tower from the main entrance in the evening

521 < Balcony above the main entrance. Above the windows of the Mayor's Hall, to the left and right coats-of-arms of the New Town and Lesser Town, in the center, above the door coats-of-arms of Vyšehrad and Hradčany, on the railing coat-of-arms of the Old Town

> 522

> 523

> 524

522 < Railing on the balcony of the façade, detail with lights
523 < Front of the balcony with lights, detail
524 < French Restaurant window
525 > Marquee above the main entrance, detail
526 > Main dome, detail
527 > Lights above the shops and a marquee above a side entrance

> 525

> 526

> 527

> 528

528 < Marquee above the main entrance, detail
529 > Municipal House and the Powder Tower

530 >> Façade

SIGHTSEEING TOURS

> 530

Profiles

Polívka, Osvald (May 24, 1859, Enns near Linz – April 30, 1931, Prague) Outstanding Czech architect from the turn of the 19th and 20th centuries, working especially in Prague. After graduation from the Technical University in Prague he gained experience under Achill Wolf and worked as an assistant to Josef Zítek, and from 1890, he worked on his own.
He collaborated with Antonín Wiehl on the construction of the neo-Renaissance Prague Municipal Savings Bank on Rytířská Street (1892–1894). Built in the neo-Renaissance style was also the Provincial Bank (today Enterpreneurial Bank – "Živnostenská banka"), which Polívka built (in 1894–1896) on Na Příkopě Street in Prague. Its technical structure was somewhat impaired in favor of its picturesqueness; the decoration was made by M. Aleš, S. Sucharda, C. Klouček, and others. Two years later, he was entrusted with the construction of the Entrepreneurial Bank ("Živnostenská banka"), opposite the Powder Tower and later pulled down, where he implemented neo-Baroque features. These features were fully developed in the construction of the Prague Municipal Savings Bank (today the Ministry of Commerce) on the Old Town Square (1899–1901), which replaced the original Baroque building. For the demolished Josefov district he designed apartment buildings on Haštalská Street. Most important are those of his buildings that were influenced by modern art: the Art-Nouveau department store U Nováků on Vodičkova Street (1902–1903), the building of Insurance Bank Prague at Národní třída, and the neighboring "Topičův dům" (1905–1907). These buildings were also decorated by renowned Czech artists, such as Jan Preisler or Ladislav Šaloun, who collaborated with Josef Mařatka on the sculptures of the New City Hall on Mariánské Square (1908–1911). Polívka collaborated with A. Balšánek on the construction of the Municipal House, where he focused mainly on the interiors. In his later works, such as the second palace of the Provincial Bank at Na Příkopě (1911–1912) with Preisler's Art-Nouveau mosaic decoration, he turned towards a more sober classicism, but with striking neo-Renaissance features. After the establishment of the Czechoslovak Republic, the 60-year-old Polívka did not strongly assert himself. However, the ornamental and bizarre character of his architectural expression still contributes to the picturesque Prague scenery.

Balšánek, Antonín (June 5, 1865, Český Brod – May 22, 1924, Prague) Architect and drawer. He studied at the Technical University in Prague, and for two years, attended drawing classes at the Prague Academy of Fine Arts (Professor A. Lhota). He traveled around Germany and Italy. He became a professor at the Czech Technical University in Prague.

His early designs bear historicizing reminiscences, and he later turned to Art Nouveau. He designed the theater buildings in Pilsen and Pardubice, the Municipal Museum in Prague (1899–1902), and various apartment buildings. He designed the decoration of the Bridge of the Legions (1901) opposite the National Theater. His work on the Municipal Museum in Český Brod and the Savings Bank in the Prague district of Vršovice can be labeled as late Art-Nouveau style. He took part in many competitions (particularly in 1910–1920), such as for the local zoning plans of the Prague Lesser Town, Hradčany, and Letná Plain, for the theater in the Vinohrady district, and for the completion of the Prague City Hall, as well as for a bridge in St. Petersburg. Among his designs, the Municipal House is the most prominent. He oversaw its construction (together with O. Polívka) from 1906 to its completion.

His drawing skills can be seen on his watercolor studies of buildings, such as of the St. Apolinaire church, or of the interior of an Orthodox church in Prague. He accompanied his studies of "Gables and Attic Gables in the Czech Renaissance" and "Summer Palace of Queen Anne at Hradčany" with illustrations (48 sketches). He left his house at Újezd (no. 8/III) to the Svatobor Club.

Aleš, Mikoláš (1852–1913) Czech painter and drawer. In 1869–1876 he studied at the Prague Academy of Fine Arts under professors M. Trenkwald and J. Sweerts. For participating in a demonstration against Professor Woltmann, who denied the existence of Czech art, he was sent to jail for four days. In 1876–1879, he worked on his friend's, Alexandr Brandeis's, farm in Suchdol. In 1879, F. Ženíšek and he won a first place in a competition for the decoration of the National Theater foyer with a project called "Winged Palette". In the same year, he left to travel and study in Italy. After his return, he lived in Prague, from where he set off on many trips to the Haná region, Slovakia, and Moravian Wallachia. Aleš belongs among the renowned 19th century Czech artists who developed J. Mánes legacy. His work, based on a combination of dramatic expression and folk insight, stayed in the shadow of the spectacular academic style of F. Ženíšek. Aleš was not allowed to carry out a cycle called "Homeland", which was his spiritual property, in the lunettes of the foyer of the National Theater. The grandiosity of his early cycles ("Senses", 1876, "Homeland", 1877–1881) and oil paintings ("Jiří of Poděbrady Meets Matyáš Korvín", 1878, "Hussite Camp", etc.) was not appreciated until his old age, when he turned to illustrations. Artistically, Aleš thought in cycles ("Elements", 1881, "Prague", 1882, "Life of the Old Slavs", 1891). He applied his sense of monumentality in many sketches for frescoes and sgraffiti on house fronts in Prague, Pilsen, and other Czech cities. He excelled as an illustrator of Czech folk songs ("Špalíček I–II", 1907, 1912), fairy tales, legends and proverbs, and books by F. L. Čelakovský and A. Jirásek. He made colored drawings for the American Bar of the Municipal House.

Kafka, Bohumil (1878–1942) Sculptor, pupil of S. Sucharda and J. V. Myslbek, worked mainly in Paris. He was a professor at the Prague Academy of Fine Arts and the School of Applied Arts in Prague, and was a member of the Société du Salon d'Automne. He concentrated mainly on symbolic works – "Dead Swan", "Life's Ruin", "Dying Stars", "Somnambulist". An impressive and dominant piece of art is his equestrian statue of Jan Žižka at Vítkov, Prague. In the entrance hall of the Municipal House are his early works – "Fauna" and "Flora".

Kalvoda, Josef (1874–1925) Sculptor, pupil of J. V. Myslbek. Before entering the Prague Academy of Fine Arts, he lived in Germany, Denmark, and Sweden. In 1903, he made a sculpture named "Merging of Souls". He created many allegorical, emotion-imbued sculptures. He made some of the sculptures for the St. Vitus's Cathedral and for the front of a bank in Moravská Ostrava. His last work "Good Shepherd" was situated in the south gardens of the Prague Castle during Plečnik's alterations. Besides other pieces, he made plaques with portraits of Czech composers for Smetana Hall of the Municipal House.

Kofránek, Ladislav (1880–1954) Sculptor, pupil of J. V. Myslbek. Traveled and studied in Germany, Holland, England, and Italy. In 1926, he made the sculptural decoration of the front of the Telephone Exchange in the Prague district of Žižkov, in 1929, the statues for the balcony of the Municipal Library in Prague, and in 1932, the sculptures for the National Bank façade in Pilsen. He decorated the front of the Faculty of Arts, Charles University, Prague, and made many portrait sculptures of prominent personalities, including a bust of Doctor Sladkovský. He contributed to the decoration of Smetana Hall of the Municipal House.

Křižík, František (1847–1941) Czech inventor and founder of an electrical firm, which, among other things, supplied special lighting units for most of the Municipal House halls. He graduated from the Technical University in Prague in electrical engineering. First he worked as a telegraph mechanic. His first invention was a railroad signal system. In 1880, he invented a differential arc lamp, which won a gold medal at the Paris World Fair in 1900 and brought him world fame. In 1891, he built the first electrical tram. The tram operated between Letná Plain and the Exhibition Ground, where the Jubilee Exhibition took place. The Jubilee Exhibition was lighted by his arc lamps and propelled by his engines, and he also presented his lighted fountain there. He was the first person in Bohemia to construct an electric car. He surpassed his age with his electric locomotives that ran between Prague and Zbraslav, and between Tábor and Bechyně.

Mára, Antonín (1877–1946) Sculptor, pupil of C. Klouček and S. Sucharda. He traveled and studied in France, Belgium, Italy, Germany, England, and Russia. In 1903, he worked under Professor Ohmann in Vienna. In 1910–1930, he was a professor in a sculpting school in Hořice. He designed the relief decoration of the building of the Main Railway Station in Prague, as well as many monuments, portraits, and coins. For the Municipal House he sculpted reliefs on the stairways to the basement and contributed to the decoration of the main façade.

Mařatka, Josef (1876–1937) Sculptor, pupil of J. V. Myslbek and C. Klouček. During his stay in Paris, he studied under A. Rodin. He introduced Rodin's works in an exhibition in 1902 and A. Bourdell's art in 1909. He was a member of the Société des Beaux Arts in Paris and a professor at the School of Applied Arts in Prague. He made many monuments (such as to the pilot M. S. Dumond) and portraits (A. Dvořák, A. Slavíček, H. Kvapilová, etc.). He created sculptures of "Music" and "Drama" for the back elevation of the Municipal House.

Mucha, Alfons (1860–1939) Czech painter, drawer and graphic artist. In his youth he worked as a decorative painter in the workshop of Kautski-Brioschi-Burghart in Vienna, and in 1881–1883, he worked as a portraitist in Mikulov. He decorated the chateau dining parlour in Hrušovany for count Khuen. He studied at the Munich Academy under professors Herterich and Löfftz. In 1888, he left for Paris, where he studied at the Julian Academy. He illustrated books and magazines, designed covers, headings, ex libris, labels, wine labels, and, especially, posters. The poster for the Theater Renaissance, announcing the performance of Gismonda, staring Sarah Bernhardt, brought him fame, and he became a very popular artist. Sarah Bernhardt signed a contract with him for six years. At the Paris World Fair in 1900, he won a silver medal and a membership in the Legion of Honor. Mucha worked at the Colarossi Academy, and later established his own school. In 1904, he left for the U.S.A., where he taught at academies in New York, Chicago and Philadelphia. At his proposal, a Slavonic Committee was established in New York. In this period, he first thought of creating a "Slavonic Epic", which he carried out after his return to Bohemia and completed in 1928 (20 huge pictures depicting the development of the Slavs, from the Svantovít celebration in Rügen to the symbolic liberation of the Slavs). The decoration of the Mayor's Hall of the Municipal House belongs among his greatest works. Mucha ranks among the most important representatives of the Art-Nouveau style. In his posters, book graphics, and decorative designs, he created masterpieces of a new decorative style.

Myslbek, Josef Václav (1848–1922) Sculptor, pupil of T. Seidan, with whom he collaborated on sculptures of military leaders for the Viennese "Arsenal", pupil of V. Levý at the Prague Academy of Fine Arts. Since 1885, he was a professor at the School of Applied Arts in Prague, and in 1896, he became a professor at the Academy of Fine Arts. Of his works most renowned are the sculptures of figures and scenes from Czech mythology for the Palacký Bridge (today they can be found at Vyšehrad), Žižka monument in Čáslav, "Devotion" on the Parliament building in Vienna, Cardinal Schwarzenberk monument in the St. Vitus's Cathedral in Prague, the equestrian statue of St. Wenceslas in Prague, and the sculptures for the Academy of Sciences in Prague. He created many portraits of prominent personalities (F. Palacký, F. L. Riegr, B. Smetana), monuments (such as of K. H. Mácha), and a sculpture of "Music" for the National Theater foyer. His "Christ on a Cross" can be found in the Sacré Coeur Basilica in Paris, and busts of F. Palacký and F. L. Riegr stand in the Municipal House in Prague.

Novák, Karel (1871–1955) Sculptor, pupil of C. Klouček. He studied at the School of Applied Arts in Prague and in J. V. Myslbek's special school. Together with sculptor J. Pekárek, he established a studio and a factory for decorative sculpture in Prague. He collaborated on the decoration of church interiors (church at Svatá Hora near Příbram, main altar and pulpit in Golešov, Silesia). He is the author of the sculpture decoration of Peterka's House, designed by J. Kotěra, on Wenceslas Square in Prague, and Hibert's House, designed by K. Hilbert, on the Masaryk Embankment in Prague. His sculptures decorate the façade of the Municipal House, for which he also created the sculptures of "Torch-bearers" on the marquee and the sculptures on the pillars in Smetana Hall.

Obrovský, Jakub (1882–1949) Painter and sculptor, he studied under E. K. Liška, S. Sucharda and M. Pirner. He traveled and studied in Italy. He became a professor at the Academy of Fine Arts in Prague. He created the decoration of the halls in the U Vejvodů House, the decorative paintings in the Pilsen brewery, two decorative panels in the Vršovice Credit Union, and the paintings for the main altar for a church in Bohnice. He exhibited his art in Venice, Rome, and Paris. He made sketches for the ceramic tiling in the Pilsen Restaurant in the Municipal House in Prague.

Pekárek, Josef (1873–1930) Sculptor, pupil of B. Schnirch, J. V. Myslbek, and C. Klouček. He was a professor at the State Technical School in Prague. He is the author of the allegory "Vltava" at the Children's Island in Prague and Wilson's medallion at the Main Railway Station in Prague. He contributed to the decoration of the Municipal House façade, he created the marble sculpture of "Nymph" for the Café, and Riegr Hall is embellished with his allegory of Prague.

Preisler, Jan (1872–1918) In 1887–1895, he studied at the School of Applied Arts in Prague under Professor F. Ženíšek. In 1906, he traveled and studied in Belgium, Holland, and Paris. In 1908–1912, he taught at the School of Applied Arts in Prague, and from 1913, he was a successor to Professor Ženíšek at the Prague Academy of Fine Arts. He was a member and chairman of the Mánes Union of Artists. Preisler was the most important personality of the founding generation of modern Czech painting. His art developed from landscape painting and Art-Nouveau symbolism to Cézanne-type pictorial structure. Later, he was influenced by E. Munch and P. Gauguin. For Palacký Hall in the Municipal House, he created the paintings on the walls and on the ceiling.

Rous, František (1872–1936) Sculptor, who, after studying and traveling abroad, lived in Prague. He ranked third in the contest for the St. Wenceslas monument in Prague. He is an author of elaborate tombstones, numerous monuments, and the decoration of the former Provincial Bank and the First Prague Credit Union. He also made monuments for Bratislava and tombstones at Olšany, and collaborated on the three-horse team for the National Theater in Prague. Many portraits of important personalities of the time and the sculpture of "Spirit of History" on the Municipal House elevation are among his achievements.

Šaloun, Ladislav Jan (1870–1946) Studied under E. Reynier, T. Seidan, and B. Schnirch. His first great success was in the contest for the decoration of the Municipal Museum in Prague, for which he sculpted the statue of "Prague" and decorated the main pediment. In 1898–1899, he made the sculptural groups "Opera" and "Drama" for a theater in Pilsen. He created many sculptures linked to architecture, such as on the former Hotel Central in Prague, the former Insurance Company building on the Old Town Square, the new Town Hall, the Main Railway Station in Prague, and the Savings Bank in Hradec Králové. He is the author of several portrait sculptures of prominent personalities on the pantheon of the National Museum. Of his numerous monuments, the best known is that of Jan Hus on the Old Town Square in Prague. He also made several monuments of T. G. Masaryk and many plaques. He made the sculptural group "Work and Science" near the gas-works in Michle, Prague. In 1927, he was named the official Prague art advisor. For the main façade of the Municipal House he created the group sculptures "Humiliation of the Nation" and "Resurrection of the Nation" and decorated Smetana Hall with his sculptures of "Slavonic Dances" and "Vyšehrad". His plaque commemorating the events of 1918 is from 1931.

Šejnost, Josef (1878–1941)
Sculptor and medalist, pupil of S. Sucharda and J. Preisler. He designed medallions with portraits of prominent personalities, artists, and politicians. He created the commemorative plaques on the homes where B. Smetana (in Litomyšl) and M. Švabinský (in Kroměříž) were born, as well as the plaque of the figures of October 28, 1918 that is placed in the Czech Club of the Municipal House. A complete collection of his medals is on display in the Pilsen museum.

Špillar, Karel (1871–1939) Painter, graphic artist and drawer. He studied at the School of Applied Arts and at the special school for decorative painting under F. Ženíšek. In 1898, he created sgraffiti for the building of the Sokol gymnasium in Nymburk and frescoes on the Credit Union in Náchod. In 1899, he decorated the pavilion of the Business Chamber of Prague for the Paris World Fair. In 1900, he designed the cover of the initial volume of the art magazine *Volné směry*. He designed many diplomas and designs for etched glass. At the beginning of the 20th century, he spent several years in Paris and Normandy. In this period, he made many pastel drawings and pictures with scenes from cafés, boulevards, and restaurants ("Palais de Glace", "Café in the Latin Quarter"). After his return, he won a contest for the mosaic decoration on the front of the Municipal House and carried out his designs for murals and ceiling paintings in Smetana Hall. Many drawings, pastel drawings, and oil paintings take inspiration from the Chod region, where he often stayed in Pec pod Čerchovem. He designed the poster for the VII Sokol Rally, "The Commemorative List of Legionnaires" and many popular ex libris.

Štrunc, Antonín (1871– unknown) Sculptor and stucco artist. In 1913, he established a company that specialized in decorative stucco art. He is the author of the stucco decoration of many important houses and public buildings in Prague: the decoration of the Savings Bank in the Vršovice district of Prague, designed by architect A. Balšánek, the façade of a school in the Karlín district of Prague, and the figural relief in the New City Hall foyer. He contributed to the decoration of the Municipal House elevation, including the allegories of "Architecture", "Sculpture", "Painting", as well as interiors, e.g., Riegr Hall.

Švabinský, Max (1873–1962) Czech painter and graphic artist. In 1891–1898, he studied at the Prague Academy of Fine Arts under Professor M. Pirner. He studied graphic art under professors J. Mařák and E. Karel. In 1897–1898, he stayed in Paris. He traveled around France, Holland, and Belgium. In 1910, he became a professor at the Prague Academy of Fine Arts, where he was the head of the graphic and figural special courses. He was an outstanding portrait artist, drawer, and graphic artist. He portrayed many prominent personalities of that time, created many monumental pieces of art (windows for the St. Vitus's Cathedral in Prague), and made designs for bank notes and postal stamps. He painted the two lunettes called "Czech Spring" in Riegr Hall of the Municipal House.

Uprka, František (1868–1929) Sculptor, brother of Jóža Uprka. He studied in the workshops of J. Čapek, A. Wagner, and B. Schnirch in Prague. He devoted his life to the folk art of his native Moravian Slovakian region. He is an author of many monuments and portrait sculptures. He participated with architect A. Balšánek on the sculptural decoration of the Credit Union in the Prague district of Vršovice. He also decorated a school in Příbor. Created a sculpture of "St. George" for the city hall in Napajedly and of a "Shepherd Girl" for the garden of the chateau Běhařov. For the rear part of the Municipal House exterior, he sculpted "Bagpiper" and "Water Fairy".

Vosmík, Čeněk (1860–1944) Sculptor, pupil of O. Wagner in Vienna. He created the pediment decoration and three reliefs for the National Museum in Prague and a sculpture of "A Man with a Bull" for the Prague slaughterhouse. He cooperated with J. V. Myslbek on the horse for the St. Wenceslas monument and on a sculptural group for the Palacký Bridge in Prague. He won a prize for "Christ in the Desert" at the Paris World Fair in 1900. He created a statue of "St. Barbora" for St. Barbora's Cathedral in Kutná Hora, a statue of "St. Ludmila" and a relief "Christ on the Cross" for the altar of St. Ludmila's Church in Prague, a sculptural group of "Two Geniuses" at the Main Railway Station in Prague, the sculpture of Matěj Rejsek on the exterior of the Municipal House in Prague, and many portraits of important personalities of the period and history (Božena Němcová, Svatopluk Čech, etc.).

Wenig, Josef (1885–1939) Illustrator, stage designer, and graphic artist. He studied at the School of Applied Arts in Prague. He illustrated fairy tales written by his brother Adolf, as well as the popular story for children called "The Bugs" by J. Karafiát. He was the main stage designer at the theater in the Royal Vinohrady district of Prague. In 1914, he painted murals in the hall of the city theater in Náchod. His decorations in the Municipal House in Prague include the decorative panels "Hop Growing" and "Viniculture" and the allegory "Prague Receiving her Guests" in the French Restaurant.

Zoula, Augustin (1871–1915) Sculptor, pupil of J. V. Myslbek. He is the author of the Karolina Světlá monument in Prague. He sculpted a relief with a Czech history topic for pavilion at the Exhibition Ground in Prague, as well as reliefs of river crafts on the lights of the Bridge of the Legions. He decorated the pantheon of the National Museum and made sculptures for the façade of the Prague Municipal Saving Bank. He participated on the decoration of the Municipal House elevation by creating the medallions with Czech folk costumes.

Ženíšek, František (1849–1916) Painter, professor at the Prague Academy of Fine Arts, member of the "Generation of the National Theater". He alternately studied in Prague and Vienna, and was a pupil of M. Trenkwald and J. Sweerts. In 1872, he shared a studio with V. Brožík. Until 1877, he collaborated with Pirner and Tulka on the designs of stained-glass windows for a votive church in Vienna. He spent the year of 1878 in Paris, and the following one in Italy. After his return, he focused on the decoration of the National Theater. The murals in the foyer of the building called "Myth", "Human Life", "History", and "National Poetry" made him famous. He decorated the ceiling of the auditorium of the National Theater with a painting, consisting of eight nymphs, symbolizing

Painting, Lyric Poetry, Pantomime, Epic, Dance, Architecture, Sculpture, and Music. He also won the contest for the decoration of the main curtain and made a colored sketch for it. Unfortunately, this first curtain was destroyed when the National Theater caught on fire in 1871. In 1880, he made sgraffiti on what is today the Smetana Museum in Prague. At the same time he painted his most famous painting "Oldřich and Božena". As a professor, he trained many competent pupils. He was a popular portrait artist, and, in 1893, he made a portrait of the emperor Franz Joseph II for the meeting hall of the Czech Academy. During his last years he created works for the pantheon of the National Museum called "Libuše's Delegation at Přemysl" and "Before his Death, St. Method Translates the Holy Scripture into the Old-Slavonic Language". The ceiling allegorical paintings, symbolizing "Life", "Poetry", and "Death" (1911), and a triptych of "Love Song", "War Song", and "Funeral Song", completed in 1914, which embellish Grégr Hall of the Municipal House, belong among his latest works.

Editor's note: the use of capitalization for individual rooms and objects is according the working standards of the Municipal House

Glossary

acanthus > a plant with prickly leaves, represented in stylized ornaments in the Municipal House

aedicule, edicula > a niche framed by two columns

allegory > a symbolic depiction of an abstract quality or idea by means of a human figure, animal, or plant

apotheosis > the deification of a person or thing

arcade > a series of arches carried on piers or columns, making an open corridor

arch ring > a walled arch of various width and molding, which strengthens the structure

architrave > the bottom horizontal part of the entablature, resting on pillar capitals

archivolt > a continuous architrave molding of the face of an arch, following its contour, sometimes just illusory

areaway > a sunken area next to a building for providing access or light and air to a basement, often with a grill

Art Nouveau > a style, which appeared around 1900, and which strives for a new artistic expression devoid of historicism, for designing the whole living environment. It is characterized by emphasizing surface, bright colors, and striking borders, and by using stylized botanical motifs. It is the last style used both in architecture and in all other kinds of art, which included also book design and applied arts. In England it is known as "Modern Style", in France "Art Nouveau", in Germany "Jugendstil", in Austria "Wiener Sezession"

balustrade > a railing consisting of small posts or pillars

bay > a part of a building that projects from the façade

bead molding > any molding composed of a string of ovoids, lenses, or half-spheres

beam > a horizontal supporting brace in the ceilings or floors

bevel, facet > a sloped edge

billet molding > a concave molding, containing short raised cylinders or rectangles

booth > a small, separated seating area

botanical > drawing inspiration from plant motifs

broach post > decorative spikes of roofs and domes

cameo > a relief picture in a gemstone

candelabrum > the wooden, stone, or metal stand of a lighting unit

cartouche > segments of different shapes with decorative borders

centerpiece > a section of ceiling, framed in a stucco molding

chambranie > the framed jamb of a window or a door

coffer > a ceiling decoration consisting of a sunken square or polygonal ornamental panel

concave > curving inward

conch > a semicircular niche surmounted by a half-dome

convex > curving outward

corbel > a projecting architectural bracket, which supports weight, such as that of a balcony or gallery

cove > a large concave molding, especially that produced by the arched junction of wall and ceiling

diamond-pointed rustication > stones of masonry blocks cut in the form of a low pyramid, used also as an ornament

dome > an evenly curved vault on a circular base

dormer window > a window placed in a sloping roof with a roof of its own

emblem > a decoration, an image with a specific symbolic meaning

entablature > a horizontal superstructure supported by columns, composed of architrave, frieze, and cornice

exedra > a larger niche, in classical architecture, a room opening full-width into a larger space

fanlight > the window over a door

fascia > a plain horizontal band, projecting slightly from the surface of a wall or in an architrave

fluting (fluted) > closely spaced parallel grooves on a column, pillar, or other surface

frieze > a decorated horizontal band

gallery > an upper story, which opens on one side to the main interior space

garland > a sculpted or painted decorative motif of flowers or fruit, finished with a ribbon, suspended in a loop

girder > a large beam that supports ceiling beams

incrustation > a layer of one material covering another material

inlay > small pieces of one material, or the same material of different color, inserted into a large piece of another, so as to create a design

lambrequin > originally a piece of fabric hung over the window or door; decorative scalloped border ornament of capitals

lesene > a vertical flat band articulating and decorating a wall, which juts from the masonry; unlike a pilaster, it does not have a decorative capital

loft > a raised area in a hall (for singers or musicians)

lunette > an area defined by a semicircle above a horizontal base

luster > one of the individual prismatic glass pendants of a chandelier

mansard > a double-sloped roof, the lower being steeper than the upper

marquee > a light roof-like structure over an entrance or a window

mascaron, mascaroon > decoration in the shape of a human face

meander > a geometrical ornament consisting of lines turning at right angles

medallion > an oval picture or relief, often with a portrait in profile

mosaic > surface decoration of floors, walls, or vaults consisting of small, colored pieces of material

octagonal > consisting of eight sides

oriel window > a window projecting from an upper story, supported on a bracket or corbel

panel painting > a panel with decorative painting filling a designated area

parapet > a low wall or railing, as along a balcony

pediment > a triangular or segmented front gable without windows

pendetive > a triangular surface of a circular area, junction between a dome and a square base

pilaster > a vertical architectural feature, projecting slightly from the wall, which often obeys the laws governing the orders of columns

pillar > a free-standing support for a part of a building, which, unlike a column, does not have to be cylindrical or conform with any of the orders

plaque > a smaller panel with bas-relief

platform > a raised area in a lecture or concert hall

polychrome > a multicolored painting of architectural or sculpted works

polygonal > consisting of several sides, angles

portal > a decorated doorway

proscenium > a stage, esp. in an ancient Greek or Roman theater

putto (pl. **putti**) > a figure of a young, male angel or cupid

relief > a sculpted composition or a design, raised above or carved into the surface

rocaille > a rococo ornament in the shape of a shell or flame

rustic > country, farm related

rustication > masonry with sculpted or textured fronts of blocks

segment > a part of a circle smaller than a semicircle

semi-pillar > the vertical half of a pillar linked to the wall or another pillar

sill > the horizontal ledge at the bottom of a window-opening or door-frame

sopraporta > a framed painting or ornament above the door

spandrel > a triangular space between an arch and its frame in arcades and portals

spherical > globular, shaped like a sphere, also concerning the celestial sphere

stained glass > colored glass panes set in lead frames

stucco decoration > sculpted decoration made of very fine plaster

stylization > emphasizing important and typical shapes

tabernacle > a canopied recess, often to contain a sculpture

tambour > a circular wall carrying a dome, often with openings to supply light

tectonic system > a system that takes into account structural needs in the decorative linking of the architectural elements of a building

terrazzo > smooth and polished flooring, consisting of a mixture of marble chips and cement

trave, bay > a section between crossbeams, as in a ceiling

trough vault > a type of vault, in which half-barrel vaults run along the width of the room

tympanum > usually triangular monumental decoration of a gable

vault > a roof based on the structural principle of the arch

voussoir > a wedge-shaped stone in an arch

wainscoting > decorative paneling of walls or ceilings, usually with wooden panels

zoomorphic > of or having animal form